Politics in Deeply Div

POLITICS IN DEEPLY
DIVIDED SOCIETIES

ADRIAN GUELKE

polity

The right of Adrian Guelke to be identified as Author of this Work has been asserted in accordance with the UK Copyright, Designs and Patents Act 1988.

First published in 2012 by Polity Press
Reprinted 2012

Polity Press
65 Bridge Street
Cambridge CB2 1UR, UK

Polity Press
350 Main Street
Malden, MA 02148, USA

ISBN-13: 978-0-7456-4849-1
ISBN-13: 978-0-7456-4850-7(pb)

A catalogue record for this book is available from the British Library.

Typeset in 10.5 on 12 pt Times
by Toppan Best-set Premedia Limited
Printed and bound in Great Britain by the MPG Books Group

The publisher has used its best endeavours to ensure that the URLs for external websites referred to in this book are correct and active at the time of going to press. However, the publisher has no responsibility for the websites and can make no guarantee that a site will remain live or that the content is or will remain appropriate.

Every effort has been made to trace all copyright holders, but if any have been inadvertently overlooked the publisher will be pleased to include any necessary credits in any subsequent reprint or edition.

For further information on Polity, visit our website: www.politybooks.com

CONTENTS

PREFACE

There are social and political divisions in all societies. But deeply divided societies are a special category of cases, in which a fault line that runs through the society causes political polarisation and establishes a force field. This divide makes establishing and sustaining democratic rule a huge challenge. The nature of such societies and the manner in which their political problems have been addressed form the subject of this book. My approach is thematic but it is linked to consideration of individual polities throughout. However, the relevance of the analysis is by no means confined to just the cases discussed in the book. This is an important consideration in the context of the political changes transforming the Middle East and North Africa, from which fresh examples of deeply divided societies seem likely to emerge.

This book has had a long gestation. I have been lecturing on the subject of the politics of deeply divided societies for most of my academic career. Initially it was as a theme in a larger Comparative Politics course, but from 1992 a module just focusing on deeply divided societies was established and has been taught at Queen's University of Belfast ever since. I owe a huge debt of gratitude to the students who have taken the module. Their critical engagement with what they were taught stimulated my own thinking. It helped that nearly all of them had expertise aplenty on the subject, simply by reason of having grown up in Northern Ireland. Another debt is owed to the numerous colleagues who have shared in the teaching of the course over the years. They include Neo Loizides, Roberto Belloni, Karin Fierke, Paul Mitchell, Amalendu Misra, Ephraim Nimni, Stefan Andreasson, and Peter McLoughlin. But a special mention must be made of Beverley Milton-Edwards. She and I previously put together a book manuscript that was intended to be a textbook for the module. This ultimately came to nothing, as each of us pursued other projects, but some of the material I contributed to that effort has proved useful as a source for this book.

Two anonymous reviewers made invaluable comments on an earlier draft and I am grateful to them for helping me to refine and to extend my analysis. I also owe a debt of gratitude to the editors and staff of Polity, including Louise Knight, David Winters and Neil de Cort. In this context, my copyeditor, Manuela Tecusan, deserves to be singled out. She did more than simply cajole me to correct errors of grammar and to unravel convoluted prose. She educated me on such issues as the etymology of irredentism. My thanks are also due to my intern from Venice, Federica Marsi, and to my wife, Brigid. They both helped me with proof-reading. However, a significant caveat applies to all these expressions of thanks. Particularly as I did not always follow the advice I was given, any failings in what follows remain solely mine.

Adrian Guelke,
Belfast,
January 2012

LIST OF TABLES

1 INTRODUCTION

Two households, both alike in dignity,
In fair Verona, where we lay our scene,
From ancient grudge break to new mutiny,
Where civil blood makes civil hands unclean.
> Shakespeare, *Romeo and Juliet*, Prologue, 1–4 (in Craig 1943: 764)

Deeply divided societies are plainly not a new phenomenon. The divisions that Shakespeare imagined in the Verona in which he set his play were based on the realities of the factionalism to be found in many a polity in medieval Europe. Indeed, Shakespeare drew on stories that were rooted in the existence of a violent political rivalry between two families that had been fought out across Lombardy. The cleavage Shakespeare described was a vertical one. Thus the Montague and the Capulet families were equal in status, as Shakespeare's opening lines make clear. But the divisions that mark deeply divided societies can also commonly be horizontal, pitting members of a subordinate community against a dominant one. And there is, similarly, no shortage of historical precedent for societies with horizontal divisions. Further, any number of examples might be given of societies where such divisions have led to conflict, going back to the great slave revolts that took place in the ancient world. Both types of deeply divided societies will be examined in this book. However, for the most part, the emphasis will be on the examination of contemporary societies, and not on how the concept of deeply divided societies might be applied in different historical contexts.

This is in part a choice made because the existing literature on deeply divided societies is about contemporary cases. In particular, the identification of deeply divided societies as presenting a special challenge to the establishment of democratic governance is comparatively new, especially insofar as the assumptions, both of the superiority of democracy over other forms of government and of its near universal feasibility, are themselves relatively recent. That is reflected in the fact that most examples of the use of the term 'deeply divided societies' in the titles of books or journal articles date from the last 40 years. Indeed, the added impetus given to the concept by the rash of ethnic conflicts that followed the end of the Cold War means that many of these works were published after 1990 (e.g. Harel-Shalev 2010; Kumar 2009; O'Flynn 2006; Al-Haj 2004). However, too much should not be made of the use of the term as a label. The problems that deeply divided societies give rise to have been a subject of debate in politics since the beginnings of political analysis, under a variety of different rubrics. Thus, in the 1920s the focus tended to be put specifically on the question of minorities in the new states of Central and Eastern Europe, but consideration of the problem of minorities raised similar sorts of issues.

At the same time, few of the books or articles that included the term 'deeply divided societies' in their titles dwelt extensively on what did or did not constitute a deeply divided society. In part that was because, with general recognition of the concept as a description for a number of conflict-ridden societies – such as apartheid South Africa, Northern Ireland during the troubles and Israel/Palestine, to give the most frequently used cases – authors conducting comparative studies of these or other similar cases did not feel the need to justify use of the term. Thus, as will be discussed below, it was writers who used the term before it came into general usage who tended to be more rigorous in how they defined the concept. This is one reason why it is worthwhile to consider the circumstances in which the term entered the general discourse of political analysis.

Classifying Democracies

A major preoccupation of political scientists in the 1950s and 1960s was the political stability of democracies, by which they meant polities in which there were regular competitive elections, generally on the basis of universal adult suffrage, and civil liberties were observed. In short, they did not include so-called people's democracies, or forms of government that used the term 'democratic' but did not meet the criteria of Western democracies – or, as they were sometimes also called, liberal democracies. The issue of what factors facilitated the stability of democracy mattered because of anxieties about the survival of democracy in a number of major

Western states, including France and Italy. These anxieties were compounded by the fact that experience of the catastrophic consequences of the failure of democracy remained fresh in people's minds. The main example in this context was the failure of the Weimar Republic and its replacement by the Nazi regime in Germany. These concerns now appear very dated and the shadow cast by the Weimar experience has long passed over.

Nonetheless, from the perspective of the immediate post-war decades, the success and durability of democracy in the United States and Britain stood in marked contrast to the experience of much of the rest of the world. The fact that, at the time, other examples of successful democracy included Canada, Australia and New Zealand simply reinforced assumptions about the superiority of the Anglo-American model. In this context, two-party systems tended to be regarded as more conducive to political stability than multi-party ones. Much of the discussion of factors favourable to the operation of liberal democracy focused on the paradox at the heart of liberal democracy: the fact that political competition was central to the effective functioning of the system, but that intense political contestation plainly represented a threat to the system. In particular, there was always the danger that the rules of the game themselves might become disputed in a democracy, leading to challenges to the legitimacy of the system and to a disinclination on the part of the losers in elections, for example, to accept the outcome of the political process. This point was central to Seymour Martin Lipset's analysis of the factors favourable to the maintenance of political stability in democracies in his seminal work *Political Man*, first published in 1959. Lipset asserted:

> Inherent in all democratic systems is the constant threat that the group conflicts which are democracy's life-blood may solidify to the point where they threaten to disintegrate the society. Hence conditions which serve to moderate the intensity of partisan battle are among the key requisites of democratic government. (Lipset 1983: 70–1)

These considerations led to a focus on the beneficial effects of factors that tended to reduce the intensity of political conflict in a democracy and to forge political consensus. Homogeneous societies were considered to be less susceptible to extremism. But, insofar as all societies contained divisions of some kind, it was considered important that these divisions should not be mutually reinforcing. Consequently, the existence of cross-cutting cleavages was seen as conducive to moderation, and hence to stability. An influential article by Gabriel Almond put forward a four-fold classification of political systems as follows:

the Anglo-American (including some members of the Commonwealth), the Continental European (exclusive of the Scandinavian and Low Countries, which combine some of the features of Continental European and the Anglo-American), the pre-industrial, or partly industrial, political systems outside the European–American area, and totalitarian political systems. (Almond 1956: 392–3)

Almond argued that, while his scheme did not encompass all existing political systems in existence at the time, it came close to doing so (p. 393).

For Almond, the key characteristic of the Anglo-American political system was 'a *homogeneous, secular* political culture' (p. 398). His other criterion was the system's 'highly differentiated' role structure. By contrast, characteristic of continental European political systems was the fragmentation of their political culture, which gave rise to a role structure in which 'the roles are embedded in the subcultures and tend to constitute separate subsystems of roles'. Almond argued that this was a product of 'an uneven pattern of development', with the consequence that there was 'in all the examples of this type of system a surviving political sub-culture'. When this occurred in combination with the existence of a communist sub-culture, the danger of immobilism in the political system existed that Almond saw as creating a threat of 'Caesaristic' breakthroughs with the potential to facilitate the emergence of totalitarianism. The potential for totalitarianism also existed in the category of pre-industrial countries, which, Almond argued, possessed mixed political cultures. Though the purpose of Almond's article was the categorisation of political systems, implicit in its analysis was the idea that conditions for the creation of stable democracies existed in relatively few societies.

The influence of Almond's article is evident from the fact that, 12 years later, the Dutch political scientist Arend Lijphart employed Almond's classification – and its further elaboration in a book Almond co-authored with G. Bingham Powell in 1966 – as the point of departure for his article on 'Typologies of democratic systems' (Lijphart 1968). What attracted Lijphart to Almond's approach was that Almond highlighted the existence of more than one form of liberal democracy, whereas most of the other current typologies of political systems of the time did not delve into the different forms that democracy might take. Lijphart did not challenge directly the empirical evidence that underscored Almond's analysis that the Anglo-American political system was associated with political stability, the continental European with unstable and weak government. But he highlighted the major problem for these correlations of deviant cases. In this context he focused on the cases that, as Almond had asserted in his

1956 article, combined features of both the Anglo-American and the continental European systems. Lijphart noted:

> All of these countries, with the exception of Austria, have multiparty systems, but they are nevertheless stable democracies. Moreover, the Benelux countries, Switzerland, and Austria have the kind of subcultural cleavage and interpenetration of parties, interest groups, media of communication, characteristic of the unstable Continental European type, but they have considerable stability; in fact, Switzerland and the Netherlands are usually counted among the most stable of the world's democracies. (Lijphart 1968: 14)

So many deviant cases, Lijphart argued, threw doubt on hypotheses that linked multi-partyism and fragmented political cultures with instability. And he underlined the strength of the sub-cultures in the cases of the Low Countries and Austria, pointing to 'the Catholic, Socialist, and Liberal *familles spirituelles* of Belgium and Luxembourg, the Catholic, Calvinist, Socialist, and Liberal *zuilen* of the Netherlands, and the Catholic, Socialist and Liberal-National *Lager* of Austria' (p. 17). He went on:

> In fact, these countries have an even more thoroughly fragmented political culture than France, Italy, and Weimar Germany, with a solid network of interpenetrating groups and media of communication within each subculture and with even less flexibility and overlapping of membership between different subcultures. One would, therefore, expect even more immobilism and instability than in the Continental European systems, but one finds just the opposite. (Ibid.).

The answer to the puzzle of these countries' record of political stability, according to Lijphart, was to be found in a combination of political leadership and institutional design. He acknowledged that, in extreme cases of fragmentation in which the population was divided into two camps with very little overlapping membership, politics tended to resemble the exchanges that might take place between two rival states, and that in these circumstances breakdown of relations and instability were not just possible but probable. However, he argued that conflict was by no means inevitable, since the leaders of the rival camps could act to counter the effect of fragmentation, especially if they were conscious of the likely consequences of their failure to do so. In this context, he gave a brief account of Austria's political development since the end of the First World War, in order to underscore his argument over the significance of political leadership. He pointed out that after the First World War there was an attempt to establish a grand coalition between the Catholic and the socialist *Lager*. However, it failed, and the ultimate consequence was a civil war, followed by dicta-torship. After the Second World War, a grand coalition was set up and ruled Austria until 1966, providing the country with the stability it had lacked between the wars.

Consociational Democracy

Lijphart identified a grand coalition, which ensured the representation in government of all of a country's major cleavages, as one in a number of aspects of institutional design that made it possible for a society with a fragmented political culture to achieve political stability, contrary to the assumptions then current among political scientists about necessary condi-tions for the long-term durability of democracy. Lijphart dubbed the systems operating in the four countries of the Netherlands, Belgium, Swit-zerland and Austria 'consociational democracy'. While he did not invent the term 'consociational', which had a long lineage, his conception of consociational democracy has become extremely influential, shaping the design of political settlements around the world, from the former Yugosla-via to Iraq and Afghanistan. The concept has proven very influential within the literature on deeply divided societies. However, it should be made clear that, in providing an account of how some of the smaller countries had achieved political stability, Lijphart was not seeking to address the prob-lems of deeply divided societies as such.

Following Almond, Lijphart categorised democracies as having a homo-geneous or a fragmented political culture. However, he considered these to be ideal types and argued that, in an empirical context,

> it is advisable to think of the criteria defining the types (categories) in terms of continua rather than dichotomies. There are no examples of either com-pletely homogeneous or completely fragmented systems; all actual democ-racies fall somewhere in between these two extremes. Similarly, there are no examples of either pure grand coalition government or pure democratic competition without any consociational features; in practice, this is a matter of degree. (Lijphart 1968: 35)

In later writings Lijphart replaced the term 'fragmented systems' with 'plural societies'. In particular, in his 1977 book *Democracy in Plural Societies*, he defined a plural society as one divided by 'segmental cleav-ages', which might be 'of a religious, ideological, linguistic, regional, cultural, racial or ethnic nature'. Further, a characteristic of these societies was that 'political parties, interest groups, media of communication, schools, and voluntary associations tend to be organized along the lines of segmental cleavages' (Lijphart 1977: 3–4).

But, while it would certainly be reasonable to argue that deeply divided societies fall within the scope of plural societies as defined by Lijphart, it is evident that his notion of a plural society encompasses a much broader range of cases than might easily be fitted under the heading of a deeply divided society. This is not surprising in the light of the importance of the case of the Netherlands in the development of Lijphart's ideas. In the same year in which his article on types of democratic systems came out, Lijphart's study of the Netherlands, *The Politics of Accommodation*, was published (Lijphart 1975). A large part of Lijphart's purpose in developing the concept of consociational democracy was to provide the basis for explaining how a society such as the Dutch had achieved its long record of internal peace and stability in spite of its social divisions. And it should be emphasised that another of the cases that Lijphart used as the basis for the formulation of his concept of consociational democracy also had a record of longstanding political stability and social peace: Switzerland. But he also intended that consociational democracy should be seen as a model for societies that had experienced violent conflict as a result of their divisions. Lijphart saw the adoption of consociational devices as offering such societies the prospect of achieving a measure of political stability and social peace despite their divisions and despite a previous history of violent conflict centred on these divisions.

Conflict Regulation

This theme was taken up by a contemporary scholar of comparative politics whom Lijphart (following Daalder) described as belonging to an 'incipient school' of consociational analysis: Eric Nordlinger (Lijphart 1977: xi). Nordlinger's book, *Conflict Regulation in Divided Societies*, was published in 1972. Despite the absence of the word 'deeply' in the title, Nordlinger established at the outset that the subject of his book was not the management of conflict in divided societies in general, but, much more specifically, 'conflict regulation in deeply divided societies featuring open regimes'. And he elaborated the point as follows: 'In studying conflict regulation in deeply divided societies featuring democratic or, more broadly, open regimes, we are searching for factors that account for the stability of such regimes under conditions of severe stress' (Nordlinger 1972: 2).

All societies, Nordlinger noted, contained class and communal divisions; but the salience that individuals tended to attach to such differences varied considerably and was inconsistent. However, in circumstances where shared understandings of these attachments prevailed and overriding importance was consistently attached to them, there was a strong potential for such social differences to give rise to segmental divisions or segments. And where such segments had a high degree of political salience, the basis existed for them to become conflict groups and to spawn conflict organisations resulting in political conflict. However, Nordlinger stressed that his interest did not extend to such political conflict in general, but only to cases where the outcome of such conflict was 'intense or severe'. In this way Nordlinger sought to narrow the focus of his study to cases he usefully dubbed 'deeply divided societies'.

The term rapidly became established in the field of comparative politics and then spread to other disciplines. As the term became embedded in scholarly discourse, the purposes for which it was used changed, with its adoption by authors whose area of study had little or nothing to do with Nordlinger's particular interest in conflict regulation. Indeed, even in the 1970s the utility of the term for societies that lay outside the realm of the open regimes Nordlinger confined himself to was recognised. A significant contribution in this context was an article in *World Politics* by Ian Lustick entitled 'Stability in deeply divided societies: Consociationalism versus control' (Lustick 1979). Lustick argued that limiting the discussion of how political stability was maintained in deeply divided societies to democratic or open regimes was unnecessarily restrictive and led to a narrow focus on the use of a number of consociational devices to facilitate political accommodation between the elites of the segments or among them (if the society had more than two segments). Lustick was interested in the various means by which dominant communities maintained their position of control in horizontally deeply divided societies, and he argued that more was involved in their exercise of control over the society than simply coercion and repression.

Lustick acknowledged the role that Nordlinger had played in establishing the currency of the term 'deeply divided societies', but his own definition of it was by no means identical to that of Nordlinger and is worth quoting. Lustick stated that he considered a society to be deeply divided

> if ascriptive ties generate an antagonistic segmentation of society, based on terminal identities with high political salience, sustained over a substantial period and a wide variety of issues. As a minimum condition, boundaries between rival groups must be sharp enough so that membership is clear and, with few exceptions, unchangeable (Lustick 1979: 325).

The largely involuntary nature of membership of a segment is a theme that recurs in much of the literature on deeply divided societies, indeed to the extent that it might be considered a characteristic feature of such societies. More generally, the issue of the definition and nature of deeply divided societies is a sufficiently important one to require examination in a separate chapter.

Organisation of the Book

The purpose of this introduction was two-fold: firstly, to set out how and why the term 'deeply divided societies' entered scholarly discourse on politics; and, secondly, to explain the organisation of the rest of the book. The first issue was addressed above. It is now appropriate to address the second. Chapter 2 seeks to clarify the characteristics of deeply divided societies. It starts by setting out as comprehensively as possible the various ways in which a society may be divided. It should be noted that not all possible sources of division are likely to lead to long entrenched or intensive political conflict. Next, consideration needs to be given to the question of what distinguishes 'deeply divided' societies from the generality of societies, all of which contain divisions of one kind or another. In this context, it should be noted that Donald Horowitz has used the term 'severely divided' society to describe the case of Northern Ireland as a way of underlining the intensity of the province's sectarian divisions and their pervasive nature (Horowitz 2001: 104–5). However, Horowitz's term has not come into general usage. Indeed it has not even displaced the widespread use of the term 'deeply divided' to describe the case of Northern Ireland.

A term that is commonly, if mistakenly, used as an alternative to 'deeply divided society' is 'ethnically divided society'. The obvious objection is that it only describes one type of deeply divided society. But, while using the term 'ethnic' limits the range of cases to be considered by specifying the nature of the division, it raises issues somewhat similar to those suggested by the concept of a deeply divided society. In particular, it begs the question of what distinguishes an ethnically divided society from one that is merely multi-ethnic in terms of the composition of its population. However, it should be conceded in this context that there are some writers who treat ethnicity as so fundamental to political life that they question the long-term viability and stability of practically all multi-ethnic societies. Their approach may be contrasted to that of Marxists, who tend to attribute a similar measure of overriding importance to divisions based upon class.

Though there are a few exceptions even on this point, most writers who use the term 'deeply divided societies' restrict its use to cases in which the divisions in question have given rise to violent conflict, or at the very least to the threat of violent conflict. In short, in the language used by Nordlinger and Lustick, there is an assumption of a high degree of antagonism between the segments into which the society is divided. And it is argued in Chapter 2 that it is characteristic of deeply divided societies that they constitute force fields in which violence, or the threat of violence, is a fundamental element in the maintenance of the society's divisions. In many cases this is underpinned by a contest for legitimacy over the nature of the political system ruling over the society.

The importance of violence and its interpretation to deeply divided societies is reflected in the themes of the next two chapters in the book. Chapter 3, drawing on the analysis in the previous chapter, examines why deeply divided societies are so prone to violence. But in this context it is argued that there are differences in the pattern of violence to be found in the two types of deeply divided societies identified above, those in which divisions between the segments are along vertical lines and those in which the divisions are horizontal, involving dominant and subordinate communities. Vertically divided societies tend to be more susceptible to 'tit for tat' violence than are horizontally divided societies. In the case of horizontally divided societies, the control exercised by the dominant community can often sustain long periods of tranquillity. But, by the same token, the crisis that follows the breakdown of control in such societies is likely to be intense and protracted. Where a single ethno-political group has established its hegemony over a multi-ethnic society, the transformation to a new regime is likely to be especially difficult. Thus Ilan Peleg argues that the transformation into democracies of such 'ethnic constitutional orders', as he has dubbed them, presents a huge challenge in a global order that has increasingly come to be dominated by the politics of identity (Peleg 2007: 14–5).

Centrality of Security

In both types of society, issues of security tend to be a source of contention and to occupy a place at or near the top of the political agenda. The consensus on questions of force and violence within the state that is commonly to be found in politically stable liberal democracies often proves elusive in deeply divided societies. The maintenance of law and order is rarely taken for granted in a deeply divided society. Indeed, communal differences tend to be sharpest on matters of security precisely because perceptions of the sources of the threat to security tend to divide along communal lines. Chapter 4 examines the issue of policing and its reform in a number of deeply divided societies, so as to highlight the problem of securing support for the means used to maintain law and order in such societies.

Chapter 5 approaches the special characteristics of deeply divided societies from another angle. It considers the ways in which other societies, including moderately divided ones, address communal differences. It focuses particularly on the processes of assimilation and integration, which reduce the salience of these differences in such societies. In this context, the chapter notes the role that political parties have played in building coalitions that cut across potential fault lines. The chapter then examines the obstacles that exist to such processes in deeply divided societies and why in particular political parties that have sought to straddle the divide in such societies have generally had limited or only temporary success. It is argued that the main reason for their failure to achieve breakthroughs is the contested legitimacy of the polity in deeply divided societies, which hampers the capacity of parties to make political appeals that are able to bridge the divide.

A consequence of the intractable nature of violent conflict in deeply divided societies is that the question is often posed as to why the polity itself should not be divided to accommodate the warring segments. This is the subject addressed in Chapter 6. Attitudes towards secession have changed radically since the end of the Cold War. Through the era of decolonisation and beyond, the major Western powers were hostile to secession as a solution to the problems of deeply divided societies, even in circumstances where the geographical distribution of the population made such an answer feasible. Fears of the Balkanisation of the African continent loomed large in the resistance to the secession of Katanga from the Congo and of Biafra from Nigeria. At the same time there was concern that legitimising secession would increase the susceptibility of new states to subversion by the Soviet Union. A more permissive attitude towards secession followed the civil wars in the former Yugoslavia and the breakup of the Soviet Union. But concerns remain that the partition of an existing territory, however brought about, tends to leave its own legacy of problems. Donald Horowitz is particularly trenchant on this issue.

> The case for partition has been argued on several grounds, only some of which are pertinent to ethnic conflict. So far as ethnicity goes, the linchpin of all the arguments is the assumption that the probable outcome of secession and partition will be more homogeneous states and, concomitantly, a lower ethnic conflict level. If the assumption were correct, the conclusion would follow. But the assumption is wrong: the only thing secession and partition are unlikely to produce is ethnically homogeneous or harmonious states. (Horowitz 2000: 589)

An obvious difficulty is that, unless partition is accompanied by partly involuntary movement of population, it tends to create new and disaffected minorities. Consequently, it is most commonly defended only as a last resort, when other possible solutions have been exhausted.

The principal alternative to the redrawing of boundaries is a settlement directed at achieving a political accommodation between the representatives of the warring segments, which is usually promoted through the use of power-sharing or other consociational devices. This is the theme of Chapter 7. In this context the role that can be played by federalism or territorial autonomy as a means to defusing conflict is also considered. But account is also taken of the criticism that has been made of consociationalism, that its pigeon-holing of populations tends to entrench divisions rather than providing societies with the capacity to reduce the political salience of communal attachments. It is argued that one of the factors favouring the use of consociational devices is the role played by external mediators. The increasing role of external mediation in the resolution of conflicts in deeply divided societies is the theme of Chapter 8. This chapter also considers the changes that have taken place in international norms that have affected the approach of the international community towards the management of conflict in deeply divided societies. These changes include the weakening of the non-intervention norm and the greater tolerance extended towards secession, which has led to a considerable increase in the number of states in the world since the end of the Cold War. The final chapter in the book summarises the findings of this study, paying particular attention to the significance attached to the problems of deeply divided societies in the context of the spread of violent conflict across international borders.

2 THE CHARACTERISTICS OF DEEPLY DIVIDED SOCIETIES

Societies may become divided in any number of different ways and many of these different cleavages may acquire a measure of political salience. However, by no means all of the sources of division in society are capable of producing – on their own, or even in combination with other sources of division – a deeply divided society. For the most part, the divisions that give rise to deeply divided societies are binary ones, since the existence of more than two groups tends to militate against the polarisation that is commonly a feature of deeply divided societies. However, there are exceptions to this general proposition. Thus Bosnia-Herzegovina remains sharply divided among the Bosniacs, Croats and Serbs, an ethnic divide rooted in religion. Before the term 'Bosniacs' came into common usage, this group was referred to as Slavic Muslims, while Croats are generally Catholics and Serbs are Orthodox. These divisions provided the building blocks of the 1995 Dayton Peace Agreement, notwithstanding the initial division of the territory between two entities, the Federation (of Bosniacs and Croats) and Republika Srpska. As Rob Aitken explains:

> The political system designed at Dayton was based on the representation of three groups recognized as the 'constituent peoples' of Bosnia-Herzegovina: Bosniacs, Serbs and Croats. The three-person Presidency consists of a Bosniac and a Croat elected from the Federation and a Serb from Republika Srpska. The House of Peoples consists of 15 delegates 'two-thirds from the Federation (including five Croats and five Bosniacs) and one-third from the Republika Srpska (five Serbs)' [Annex 4, Article 1, paragraph 1 of Dayton Peace Agreement]. A majority of delegates from any constituent people have

a veto over parliamentary decisions. The other chamber, the House of Representatives, is directly elected two-thirds from the territory of the Federation and one-third from the territory of the Republika Srpska. (Aitken 2010: 238)

Another example of a society with a three-fold division is Iraq. Just how deep were the country's divisions among Shi'a Arab Muslims, Sunni Arab Muslims and Kurds became apparent after the overthrow of Saddam Hussein's autocratic regime in 2003. In this case the divisions are rooted in both sectarian and ethnic differences, with sectarianism the basis of the Sunni-Shi'a divide and a distinctive ethnic identity setting Kurds apart from other Iraqis. One of the main objectives of Iraq's 2005 constitution was to provide an institutional basis for accommodating these differences in ways that John McGarry and Brendan O'Leary describe as 'consistent with liberal consociational principles' (McGarry and O'Leary 2008: 347). The converse of the proposition that not all cases of deeply divided societies have a single fault line dividing two groups is that not all binary divisions can produce deeply divided societies. Thus gender is a binary category, but, while gender certainly is not without significance as a factor in the politics of most societies, a society deeply divided on the basis of gender is practically speaking inconceivable.

At the outset it might seem that some types of cleavage are more likely to produce a deeply divided society than others. And this is reflected in the literature in a tendency to equate ethnically divided societies and deeply divided societies. While there is a measure of overlap between the two categories, by no means all deeply divided societies are primarily ethnically divided societies. It is therefore worth considering first the main types of cleavage, before examining whether and in what circumstances they might give rise to a deeply divided society. The following remain relatively common sources of division in societies around the world: class, caste, religion, language, race, ethnicity and clan. To these the following binary divisions can be added: settler versus native; immigrant versus indigenous population; pastoralist versus cultivator; peasant versus landowner; urban versus rural; and centre versus periphery. A further source of division that has emerged in recent years has been the prior experience of being ruled by a different polity or under a different political system. It is worth expanding on each of these in turn.

Class and Caste

Complicating the evaluation of class as a source of division is the primary role accorded to it in the interpretation of politics by Marxists. One consequence is that, when it comes to the analysis of individual cases, there tends to be a lack of consensus among scholars on the significance that ought to be accorded to class. And there is often considerable debate, too, on the role to be accorded to class in reinforcing or underpinning other cleavages. However, even scholars who reject Marxism as an interpretative framework for understanding conflict accept that there are cases of societies that have been deeply divided on the basis of class. Austria between the First and the Second World War, the era of the country's First Republic, provides one such example; Chile in the early 1970s another. Since the end of the Cold War, the importance of class as a basis for political mobilisation has diminished, in step with the waning of communist or socialist alternatives to capitalism and to globalisation. Admittedly, it is possible that the impact of the global economic downturn may sharpen class antagonisms, as living standards fall and the level of unemployment continues to rise in the most adversely affected countries. How such antagonisms might manifest themselves is another matter. One possibility might be an increase in hostility towards immigrants, and not necessarily a revival in the fortunes of the left. In this context, the increasing success of right-wing populist parties across Europe has already attracted considerable attention in the media (Scally 2011).

Caste is commonly associated with India and with the practices of the Hindu religion. The essence of the Hindu caste system is that people are born into a particular occupational group with a predetermined position in the social hierarchy. Despite the fact that the Indian constitution outlaws discrimination on the basis of caste, and despite governmental policies designed to undo the impact of the caste system on social stratification through affirmative action, the system survives in various forms. Further, the issue of relations between different castes remains a potent influence on politics, though mainly at state level rather than nationally. State elections in Uttar Pradesh in 2007 provide a relatively recent example of the influence of the caste system on politics. In these elections the Bahujan Samaj Party won a remarkable victory through the forging of a rainbow coalition between upper-caste Brahmins and low-caste Dalits (Ramesh 2007). However, while the caste system is associated in India with violence and intimidation, which tend to be directed at those at the bottom of the social hierarchy, the very complexity of the system has prevented it from becoming a primary axis of conflict. But outside India caste or caste-like divisions have rarely been the source of major conflict in society.

The most striking exceptions are the cases of Rwanda and Burundi. Generally speaking, the division in the two societies between Hutus and Tutsis is characterised as a conflict between ethnic groups. But, with the origins of the two groups in the segmentation of the two societies on horizontal rather than vertical lines, between upper-caste pastoralists and low-caste cultivators, caste rather than ethnicity provides the more accurate characterisation of the divide. The severe conflicts, including episodes of genocide, that have occurred in both Rwanda and Burundi between the Tutsi minority and the Hutu majority over a period of more than fifty years make both cases clear-cut examples of deeply divided societies.

Religion and Sectarianism

Religion remains a common source of division. It takes a wide variety of forms and takes place at various levels. Huntington's prediction that the ending of the ideological divide in the world as a result of the collapse of the Soviet Union might be followed by a clash of civilisations has focused particular attention on the potentiality for conflict between Christians and Muslims (Huntington 1993). Added verisimilitude was given to these concerns by the events of 11 September 2001, when supporters of Osama bin Laden launched simultaneous mass casualty attacks on the United States in the name of a global jihad. But this is at the international level. There are relatively few societies in the world that contain proportionally large numbers of both Christians and Muslims. One exception is Nigeria. From time to time, fears have arisen of the country's division on the basis of the fault line between the Muslim North and the Christian South. Following the victory of the incumbent, Goodluck Jonathan, in the country's presidential election of 2011, more than a thousand people were killed in post-election violence, particularly in the North, the stronghold of the opposition (Nossiter 2011). A factor in the conflict was the contention of the opposition that Jonathan's election violated a commitment to alternation in presidential rule between the Muslim North and Christian South. However, as the terms in which this is discussed underscore, the divide has a regional as well as a religious dimension. Further, other sources of cleavage in Nigeria, including ethnicity, have tended to limit the impact of the purely religious divide.

Even in societies in which one religion has been predominant, conflict has occurred, but the pattern has not been conflict at the national level between Christians and Muslims, but rather conflicts within particular regions of countries in which one or the other faith tends to predominate. An example is predominantly Muslim Indonesia, where there have been serious episodes of violence between Muslims and Christians in particular regions. At the turn of the century, from 1999 to 2002, the Maluku Islands (also known as the Moluccas or Spice Islands) were afflicted by violence between Muslims and Christians in which approximately 9,000 people died and 400,000 fled their homes. A peace accord following the intervention of the central government put an end to the fighting in 2002 (Schulze 2002: 57).

The main example of a country that has been severely affected by conflict between Christians and Muslims, most notably during the bloody civil war between 1975 and 1990, is Lebanon. It is an important case, as Lebanon has long been seen as a prime example of a deeply divided society. It was also seen as a leading example of the use of consociational devices to ensure the functioning of democratic institutions in spite of the country's divisions. Lebanon's National Pact at the time of the country's independence in 1943 established the basis for its consociation. Lebanon was one of the six cases chosen by Nordlinger to illustrate his theme of conflict regulation in deeply divided societies, while it also featured prominently in Lijphart's voluminous writings on consociationalism. However, by the time of the publication of Lijphart's *Democracy in Plural Societies* (1977), Lebanon was engulfed in civil war, so Lijphart was forced to address the failure of its consociation. He did so by defending the record of consociationalism as having given the country more than 30 years of democratic stability in a turbulent region of the world, but he also identified as a weakness of the Lebanese system its overly rigid allocation of positions in government on the basis of an outdated census, an arrangement that was not subject to change and that contributed to the system's immobilism (Lijphart 1977: 147–50).

It should also be emphasised that Lebanon was by no means a straightforward case of a society divided between Christians and Muslims. Sub-divisions of the country's major faiths have played an important role, with Christians divided among Maronite, Greek Orthodox and Greek Catholic branches and Muslims divided among Sunnis, Shi'as and Druze. In addition, the presence of large numbers of Palestinian refugees was a factor exacerbating conflict between the Christian and Muslim blocs in the early 1970s. And a further element that contributed to the political destabilisation of Lebanon before and through the course of its civil war was military intervention in its affairs by the country's neighbours, Israel and Syria.

Other examples might be given where communal divisions coincide with the presence of adherents of two of the world's major religious faiths. Thus the divide in Cyprus might be conceived of as one pitting Greek Orthodox Christians against Muslims, the divide in Sri Lanka as pitting Buddhists against Hindus; but in both cases religion is not the primary source of the division and its role as a cause tends to be downplayed. A case where it is more difficult to dismiss the role of religious divisions per se is inter-communal conflict in India between Hindus and Muslims. But its episodic nature, as well as Hindu predominance in the country as a whole, has prevented this cleavage from dominating the country's politics to the point that the vast country of India could be described as a deeply divided society in its own right. However, it is possible to describe particular regions of India, such as the state of Jammu and Kashmir, as deeply divided.

Conflict also occurs between different branches of the same faith, and there are a number of places in which these sectarian differences are a source of division. The most obvious case of a society divided along sectarian lines is Northern Ireland. Yet even though the conflict has been most commonly, as well as accurately, described as one between Protestants and Catholics, it can be argued that, since what has divided the society has little to do with religious doctrine, religion should be seen simply as a marker of ethnic or national differences. And that is widely reflected in the literature in the characterisation of Northern Ireland as an ethnically divided (as well as a deeply divided) society. The conflict between Sunni and Shi'a Muslims in Iraq since the overthrow of Saddam Hussein is another instance of a society divided along sectarian lines, but in this case it cannot be argued that religion is a marker of different national identities. However, politics in American-occupied Iraq has not been entirely dominated by the country's sectarian divide, not least because of the further complication of the Kurdish question. Lastly, religion has provided a source of division even in societies in which religious observance has been largely confined to a single branch of one of the major religions. In particular, in Catholic countries such as France, Spain and Italy considerable tensions have arisen from time to time between clerical and anticlerical forces.

Language and Race

Another major source of division in a number of societies is language. Examples are the divide between Dutch-speaking Flemings and French-speaking Walloons in Belgium; between anglophones and francophones in Canada, primarily centred on the province of Quebec; and between German speakers and Italian speakers in South Tyrol, on the border between Italy and Austria. As in the case of some of the conflicts involving religion, language may be seen simply as a marker of ethnic difference and the situation characterised as an ethnic conflict. In acknowledgement of the role of language as a marker of the divide, the term 'ethno-linguistic cleavage' is also in common usage. Among the cases mentioned above, that of Belgium has received the most attention. It was one of the six cases that

Nordlinger examined under the deeply divided societies rubric. It was also one of the four cases of small European states on which Lijphart based his theory of consociational democracy. However, as Nordlinger noted in his 1972 study, the sources of Belgium's divisions have varied over the years.

> Belgium was faced with a severe church–state conflict from the time of its creation in 1830 to 1958; between 1880 and 1920 it experienced a sharp class conflict; and from the 1950s to the present, Belgium has been racked by a highly charged linguistic–territorial conflict between Flemings and Walloons. (Nordlinger 1972: 18)

In other cases, too, the importance attached to language as a part of ethnic or national identity has by no means been constant. Thus the promotion of the Irish language was not a high priority for Irish republicans seeking a united Ireland in the 1970s. The hunger strike crisis in the early 1980s boosted interest in the language in large part because of its use by prisoners. And political circumstances may even determine the form that a particular language takes. The creation of Yugoslavia facilitated the development of Serbo-Croat as a lingua franca for the country, while its dissolution brought about the deconstruction and replacement of this language as a means of communication transcending ethnic differences.

Race based on observable physical differences among human beings such as skin colour is another significant source of division. Even more than language and religion, race tends to be conflated and confused with ethnicity. This is in part because both in the United States and in the United Kingdom the term 'ethnic minorities' is used in governmental publications as an acceptable way of referring to racial groups in a context in which the concept of race itself is being questioned. Thus in the United Kingdom a reference to ethnic minorities is generally understood to be to people with Asian, African or Caribbean backgrounds rather than, say, to people from Scotland or Wales. Referring to racial cleavages using the language of racial differences presents the problem that to do so is open to the misinterpretation that racial categories are being validated in the process. Further, groups that suffer racial discrimination may also prefer ethnic self-description precisely as a way of avoiding inadvertently lending credence to racial stereotypes. An obvious example is the currency of the term African Americans. It corresponds to usage of terms such as Irish American and Italian American.

Another country where the conflation of race and ethnicity is apt to cause confusion is South Africa. Under apartheid, the government did its utmost to promote ethnic differences among the indigenous African population as a divide-and-rule strategy. It largely failed in its efforts as has been underlined in successive elections in the country since the end of apartheid. The appeal of ethno-nationalist parties to the African electorate has proved weak, with the African National Congress (ANC) as the overwhelming choice of most African voters. However, racial divisions have not disappeared and the correlation between race and voting behaviour remains strong.

Ethnicity

It is difficult to overstate the importance of ethnicity as a factor in the creation of deeply divided societies. This is because, although there are many other potential sources of division in society, as has been discussed above, ethnic cleavages are especially prone to lead to political conflict. Important in this context is the connection between ethnicity and nationalism in the form of ethno-nationalism. Ethnicity is not easy to define. The term 'ethnic' originates in the ancient Greek word *ethnos*. It can loosely be translated as 'tribe' or 'nation', but with the qualification that it applies to other people and is not a self-description. This implication has been retained in translations into modern languages. As Lincoln Allison has put it, 'ethnicity remains one of the most elusive and mysterious aspects of social structures but also one of the most fundamental and important' (Allison 2003: 178). Part of the difficulty in tying down ethnicity as a concept is the mix of objective and subjective criteria that underpin it.

In this context, Hutchinson and Smith draw a useful distinction between an ethnic community or *ethnie* and an ethnic category. The second requires only that there is a perceived cultural difference between the group and outsiders and the identification of a boundary around the group. This perception may originate outside the group itself, and the group may even owe the name accorded to it as an ethnic group to outsiders, as was the case with the description Eskimos, now largely discarded for that reason. Hutchinson and Smith provide a much more elaborate definition of ethnic community as having, to varying degrees, six main features. They list them as follows:

1   a common *proper name*, to identify and express the 'essence' of the community;
2   a myth of common *ancestry*, a myth rather than a fact, a myth that includes the idea of a common origin in time and place and that gives an *ethnie* a sense of fictive kinship, what Horowitz terms a 'super-family';

3 shared *historical memories* or better, shared memories of a common past or pasts, including heroes, events and their commemoration;
4 one or more *elements of common culture*, which need not be specified but normally include religion, customs and language;
5 a link with a *homeland*, not necessarily its physical occupation by the *ethnie*, only its symbolic attachment to the ancestral land, as with diaspora peoples;
6 a sense of solidarity on the part of at least sections of the *ethnie*'s population (Hutchinson and Smith 1996: 7).

Some ethnic communities or *ethnies* remain highly durable and their origins can be traced back hundreds of years, but there is also a constant process of the rise and fall of ethnic communities. That is reflected in the disappearance of groups such as the Scythians, the Philistines and the Etruscans. And over time groups may combine, as well as divide, leading to the creation of new groups. The importance that individuals accord to their ethnic identity varies considerably and is highly dependent on context. And it may be of lesser significance than other identities that individuals possess. Consequently the fact that a society contains individuals with different ethnic identities is not in itself divisive or a cause of conflict. Clearly, what matters is when and why ethnic identities become politicised.

As in the case of class, scholars are divided in their view on the role of ethnicity in political conflict. Broadly speaking, there are two contrasting perspectives on this issue: primordialism and instrumentalism. John Rex has provided succinct descriptions of the two positions. He describes as the essence of primordialism that 'ethnic bonds are quite unlike all others; they are recurrent, largely inexplicable, and have an overpowering emotional and non-rational quality', while he characterises instrumentalism as follows: 'they [ethnic bonds] are, if not wholly invented by political leaders and intellectuals for purposes of social manipulation, at least related to specific social and political projects' (Rex 1997: 271). Whereas primordialists regard ethnicity as an intrinsic and fundamental aspect of social life and view its politicisation in that context, instrumentalists are inclined to see ethnicity as an element that is manipulated and socially constructed for the purpose of political mobilisation. From either perspective it is possible that ethnicity will give rise to division and to conflict.

Historically, clans have been a cause of division in many societies. In Chapter 1 the fictional example of the Montagues and the Capulets – based on real family rivalries in medieval Italy – was mentioned. Another striking example is provided by the feud between the Campbells and the MacDonalds in the Scottish Highlands, which dated from the Glencoe massacre at the end of the late seventeenth century. But the reason for including the category of clan is not cases from the distant past, but its emergence as a factor in contemporary politics in one of the few ethnically homogeneous societies on the African continent, Somalia. In the anarchic conditions that have prevailed in that country since the end of the Cold War, clans have emerged as an important factor in filling the political vacuum. In particular, in the early 1990s the collapse of the Siad Barre regime was followed by a power struggle between clan warlords in which thousands of people were killed.

Binary Divisions

Let us now consider some binary divisions that may give rise to political conflict. In many cases these overlap with the categories discussed above. The division of society into settlers and natives as a legacy of colonisation or conquest is a pattern to be found in many parts of the world. As a potent basis for the polarisation of society, it is strongly associated with the concept of deeply divided societies. Thus three of the most widely cited examples, South Africa, Israel/Palestine and Northern Ireland, have all been characterised in such terms (Mitchell 2000). Admittedly, the characterisation is controversial because of the implication of the illegitimacy of settler rule and because of the longevity of the settler presence, which in the case of Northern Ireland and South Africa can be traced back to the sixteenth and the seventeenth century respectively. And there are ready-made alternatives available. The division of a society into settlers and natives can almost always be categorised in either racial or ethnic terms. It is also almost invariably a horizontal division, with the settlers forming the dominant community.

However, situations in which both settlers and natives constitute substantial proportions of the population of the same polity are today relatively rare. In some cases the settlers displaced the indigenous population, so that the proportion of the population descended from the society's inhabitants prior to colonisation is small, as for example in the cases of the United States of America, Canada and Australia. In others, settlers formed too small a proportion of the population to be able to hold on to power after decolonisation. Smith's Rhodesia was one of the last cases of a polity based explicitly on rule by a settler minority. It finally succumbed in 1980. South Africa, which achieved majority rule in 1994, might be considered another. But it is not a straightforward case, not least because the main opposition movement to apartheid, the ANC, rejected the categorisation of the society in these terms. The ANC characterised its struggle as one directed at replacing apartheid with a non-racial democracy. By contrast, its rival, the Pan-Africanist Congress (PAC), with its notorious slogan of 'one settler, one bullet', did present the conflict as about the overthrow of settler rule, but its popular appeal proved very limited, not least because of fears of a racial bloodbath if this approach was heeded.

The issue of immigration looms large in the politics of many countries, but only in a handful of cases are there large enough numbers of immigrants for the divide between immigrants and the indigenous population to be the source of a major cleavage. A notable exception is Fiji. The islands contain substantial numbers of both indigenous Fijians and Indo-Fijians, the descendants of indentured labourers brought from India in the last decades of the nineteenth century to work in sugar plantations after Fiji became a British colony in 1874. The demographic balance between the two groups has shifted over time and this shift has been one factor in fuelling tensions. In 1987 Indo-Fijians narrowly outnumbered indigenous Fijians (Premdas 1995: 9). However, by the time of the census in 2007, the balance had shifted decisively back in favour of indigenous Fijians. According to that census, indigenous Fijians comprised 57 per cent of the population, compared to 37 per cent for Indo-Fijians (Fiji Islands Bureau of Statistics 2008). The change reflected in part emigration by Indo-Fijians in response to the islands' political instability after 1987.

Fiji achieved independence in 1970. Its political instability dates from 1987, when the victory of the Fijian Labour Party in the country's general election prompted a military coup on the grounds that the new government, which drew its support overwhelmingly from Indo-Fijians, represented a threat to the interests and rights of the indigenous population. The military government then amended the constitution to entrench the supremacy of indigenous Fijians. In particular, indigenous Fijians were guaranteed an overall majority of the seats in the House of Representatives under a system of communal representation. But after negative reaction internationally, a fresh constitution was introduced in 1997 that was the product of extensive negotiations between representatives of indigenous Fijians and Indo-Fijians. However, its implementation proved fraught with difficulty, and there were further coups and attempted coups from 2000 on. After a period of political instability, the military under Frank Bainimarama seized power in December 2006. Commodore Bainimarama has promised to introduce a constitution without ethnic provisions in 2013 and elections in 2014. Fiji was suspended from the Commonwealth in 2009.

There are widely differing interpretations of the centrality of the division between indigenous Fijians and Indo-Fijians, especially in the light of significant differences among indigenous Fijians themselves (Lawson

1990: 797). Another notable feature of scholarship on Fiji has been the debate over the contribution that constitutional design might make to the resolution of the conflict. A key element of the 1997 constitution was the adoption of the alternative vote method of election in the 1997 constitution, alongside provisions for power-sharing between the representatives of the two communities. The theory behind the creation of open seats employing the alternative vote was that it would encourage moderation and inter-ethnic co-operation.

> As the winning candidate must secure at least 50 percent of the votes plus one, which few candidates or parties would be able to muster from their own community, each party would have an incentive to enter into arrangements with another party to trade their second-order preferences. In due course, this type of cooperation would lead to multiethnic or non-ethnic parties, and facilitate national unity and a broader national agenda. (Ghai and Cottrell 2008: 302)

However, the potential impact of the alternative vote system was much reduced by the decision that only a minority of the seats would be open ones. The majority of seats remained the preserve of one community or the other. Further, as Ghai and Cottrell note, in practice the open seats and the alternative vote system made little difference to the continuing polarisation of opinion along communal lines after 1997. At the same time, they point to similar polarisation under other consociational settlements, including in Northern Ireland (p. 312). In view of the fact that Northern Ireland used a different electoral system but had a comparable outcome, the implication was that the choice of electoral system had little capacity to transform politics in any of these societies. And a fair conclusion would be that none of the cases debated in the literature provides conclusive evidence as to which electoral system might prove optimal in a deeply divided society.

A factor in exacerbating both conflicts between indigenous and immigrants and those involving settlers and natives is the importance that tends to be attached to who came first or who occupied the land originally. Greater political legitimacy tends to be accorded to groups that can make a convincing claim for their historical precedence. This is reflected in the importance attached by settler communities to narratives that dispute the claims of natives to prior occupation, as in the famous description of Israel in the early twentieth century as 'a land without a people for a people without a land'. In the case of South Africa, a myth propagated to legitimise white rule was that, at the time when the Dutch established a settlement at the Cape, Bantu-speaking Africans were only just arriving in the area that eventually became the territory of the Union of South Africa. This myth was eventually debunked by archaeological evidence that proved much earlier Bantu-speaking occupation.

One of the most famous songs in the musical *Oklahoma* makes the plea that 'the farmer and the cowman should be friends'. The context is conflict between the interests of ranchers and farmers in the United States. Though the divide between pastoralists and cultivators never had the potential to develop into a major cleavage in American society, it was, nonetheless, a significant source of division in some parts of the country prior to industrialisation. A contemporary example of violent conflict between pastoralists and cultivators can be found in the Darfur region of Sudan. Ironically, the rebellion in Darfur followed the signing of a peace treaty in Sudan's long-running civil war between the Arab North and the African South in 2002. In the aftermath of the uprising in Darfur the central government gave its support to nomadic militias known as the Janjaweed, in an effort to quell the rebellion. As referred to above, the conflicts in Rwanda and Burundi can also be described as arising from divisions that had their origin in a cleavage between pastoralists and cultivators that had taken on a caste dimension. By contrast, the clash of interests between the two groups in the Darfur region in relation to access to scarce resources such as water might reasonably be represented as a species of class conflict. In fact, the countryside of the world is beset by class conflict in a number of different forms.

The divide between landowners and peasants in the Third World was a significant source of conflict in the decades immediately following the Second World War. The appeal of land reform was central to a number of communist insurgencies, including the revolutions in Vietnam, Laos and Cambodia. The issue fuelled guerrilla warfare from Nepal to Peru. Even after the end of the Cold War, landlessness has continued to be a cause of conflict in particular regions in a number of countries across the Third World. For example, Gutierrez and Borras argue in a 2004 policy paper that it is an identifiable element in the conflict in Southern parts of the Philippines (Gutierrez and Borras 2004), though this conflict is more commonly categorised in religious terms, given the Muslim religious identity of the insurgents in a predominantly Catholic country. As this example underlines, a social fault line may be reinforced by the combination of a number of lines of division that reinforce each other. The divide between the interests and perspectives of people living in rural and in urban areas is widely reflected in voting behaviour, with the appeal of different parties to rural and urban constituencies varying considerably. But these differences are generally ones of degree. In exceptional cases, sharp political polarisation between rural and urban areas can arise. A contemporary example is Thailand, where the former prime minister,

Thaksin Shinawatra, retains overwhelming support in the rural areas, despite being forced from office; and this has been demonstrated very clearly by the electoral triumph of his sister, Yingluck Shinawatra, in the country's elections in 2011 (Fuller 2011).

The conceptualisation of politics in spatial terms as pitting the centre against the periphery can be seen either as a general theory about the location of power or simply as a reflection of the fact that political alignments tend to be forged around the issue of involvement in the decision-making process; and this is unevenly distributed. Those on the geographical periphery commonly feel remote from decision-making and consequently excluded from power. The duality of centre versus periphery can be applied both to the distribution of power within the international political system and to relations that exist among the different regions of individual states. It can also be applied to entities such as the European Union (EU), with Germany at the centre and countries such as Greece and Ireland on the periphery. The crisis of the single currency has given added weight to this distinction. In terms of politics within states, the potency of this division tends to be greatest where reinforced by other cleavages. The uneven impact of globalisation has tended to sharpen the role of this spatial dimension. For example, in the United Kingdom the Conservative Party has become increasingly a party of the centre, with little representation in the House of Commons outside of England.

The last division to be considered is the imprint left by rule as a separate polity (or as part of another polity). The impact on people's identity of being members of the same polity, even if not exercising democratic rights within that polity, is surprisingly durable. Added weight was given to this factor by the international norm that stipulated that political entities that had been ruled over as colonies were entitled to independence in terms of their existing boundaries. It is notable that Indonesia, which took over the former Portuguese colony of East Timor with the encouragement of Henry Kissinger in 1975, was unable to win over the population to its rule, with the ultimate consequence that East Timor was able to re-emerge as an independent state following the collapse of the Indonesian dictatorship. Somalia became an independent state in 1960 through the merger of former British and Italian colonies. Despite the new entity's ethnic homogeneity, the imprint left by different experiences of colonial rule endured and in the 1990s the territory that Britain had ruled as the protectorate of Somaliland resurfaced, declaring its independence from the rest of the country in 1991.

A perhaps even more surprising example is that of reunified Germany. Though the partition of Germany lasted less than half a century and the legitimacy of communist rule remained in question throughout the period of the existence of East Germany, differences between the West German-originating majority of the population and those from the East, the Ossies, have persisted and are reflected in different voting behaviour among the Ossies, who provide the bulk of support for the left political party (Die Linke) but form the basis of a widely perceived social divide (Paterson 2009). The seriousness of the divide should not be overstated. In particular, it has not led to political violence and does not pose a threat to the country's political stability. Nonetheless, the expectation after reunification was that the integration of the two parts of Germany and the measures taken to address the legacy of communist rule in the East would lead to the erasure of differences among Germans based on their experience of the post-war decades. This has not come to pass. Indeed, it has been confounded by the very evident persistence of this fault line and by continuing political sensitivity over the issue in contemporary Germany.

Polarising Differences

Hitherto in this chapter various ways in which a society may become divided have been discussed. It is not suggested that the discussion has by any means exhausted the possibilities. Indeed, some quite obvious sources of social division, such as lifestyle and age, have not been touched on. This is because the focus was on divisions that might polarise a society politically and thereby create the basis for a deeply divided society. In the process, examples of deeply divided societies were identified. However, the issue of the distinguishing characteristics has yet to be addressed. It is worth in this context considering what other authors have identified as the special features of deeply divided societies.

As has already been noted, it is common, in the literature, for deeply divided societies to be equated with ethnically divided ones. Though the term 'ethnic' might be stretched to cover some of the divisions considered above, there are quite a number of cases of deeply divided societies where ethnicity is not the basis of the fault line between the communities. One of the most commonly cited cases of a deeply divided society, South Africa, was and is deeply divided on the basis of race rather than ethnicity. Admittedly, it might be objected that race and ethnicity are closely related concepts. And it may be difficult to draw a sharp distinction in some situations and contexts where they overlap. However, in the South African case, the difference is sufficiently clear-cut to make it possible to conclude that hitherto post-apartheid South Africa has confounded predictions that ethnicity would be a source of division among the African majority – predictions that were current prior to apartheid's demise. In any event, South

Africa is far from being the only reason for rejecting what might be called the ethnic view of what constitutes a deeply divided society. To give another example, interwar Austria was divided to the point of civil war on the basis of class. And the major cleavage in contemporary Iraq between Shi'as and Sunnis rests on a sectarian and not an ethnic fault line. Admittedly, the divide with the country's Kurds is best characterised as an ethnic one, which demonstrates that different types of cleavage can exist in parallel in the same society without their political salience necessarily being reduced through the creation of cross-cutting cleavages.

Unsurprisingly, there is also a tendency in the literature for authors to derive their view of what constitutes a deeply divided society from the particular case or cases they focus upon. For example, in his book on the South African transition, Tim Sisk argues that what made South Africa a deeply divided society was its rigidly imposed identities under apartheid and its high degree of inequality (Sisk 1995). But a little reflection will demonstrate that neither of these two criteria is in practice of much help in distinguishing the features of deeply divided societies. Thus the very clear lines of segmentation on the basis of language in Switzerland provide little reason for considering this affluent country a deeply divided society, notwithstanding its inclusion among Lijphart's example of consociational democracies. Nor is inequality a useful criterion in the context of seeking to identify deeply divided societies. In terms of the distribution of income and wealth, Brazil has numbered for many years among the most unequal societies in the world, yet Brazil is not generally considered to be a deeply divided society. And, for that matter, Northern Ireland, which has long been seen as an archetypal example of a deeply divided society, is not an especially unequal society in terms of the distribution of income and wealth.

In Chapter 1 Lustick's definition of a deeply divided society was quoted. He argued that a society might be considered deeply divided 'if ascriptive ties generate an antagonistic segmentation of society, based on terminal identities with high political salience, sustained over a substantial period and a wide variety of issues' (Lustick 1979: 325). The term 'ascriptive' generally tends to be applied to identities acquired at birth, such as race or ethnicity, though it might be applied to a wider set of identities, depending on the society in question. But, as discussed above, the fact that a society can be deeply divided in class terms, even in modern societies in which mobility between classes is possible, is an argument against including 'ascriptive ties' as an essential criterion. A stronger argument can be advanced for Lustick's two other criteria: firstly, that the term should be limited to cases of sustained division along a particular fault line; and, secondly, that the fault line should be seen as having overriding importance, so that its influence extends over a wide range of issues facing the society.

Almost any society may become polarised over a particular government policy, such as military intervention in another country, major public sector projects such as the building of a motorway or an airport, or emotive issues such as the export of live animals for slaughter. And it is possible for such issues to cause a major political crisis and to generate acts of lethal political violence. However, generally speaking, such crises tend to be short-lived and to have a limited impact upon voting behaviour or political alignments. Admittedly, this tends to be clearer in retrospect than it may be in the midst of crisis. The war in Algeria was a factor in the political instability of the French Fourth Republic, which in turn helped to underscore the negative view of political scientists of the continental European model of democracy. However, once the question of Algeria had been resolved by President de Gaulle – albeit under a new regime: the French Fifth Republic – the issue lost its importance as a source of division and immobilism. Similarly, the student revolt of May 1968 appeared at the time to signal a massive crisis in the very existence of the French Fifth Republic, but ultimately it did not lead to far-reaching political change either in the institutions of government or in the party system.

Lustick's other criterion, that it is a characteristic of deeply divided societies that their major cleavage affects a wide range of issues, is an insightful one. The tendency in such societies for all political issues to be viewed through the prism of their impact on the society's principal fault line undercuts the operation of the cross-cutting cleavages that moderate conflict in most societies. And such a tendency effectively prevents the formation of political coalitions on issues that cut across the main societal divide. The case of Northern Ireland provides many examples of the dominant role of its main cleavage in determining political alignments on matters seemingly unconnected to the struggle between Protestants and Catholics over the entity's constitutional destiny. A striking illustration is how the society has polarised along sectarian lines on the issue of the Middle East conflict. In 2002, when Ariel Sharon launched his assault on the Palestinian Authority, his action prompted the flying of literally thousands of Israeli flags on lamp-posts in Protestant neighbourhoods, so scarcely any lamp-posts remained unfestooned. At the time the display underlined unionist preference for Sharon's military approach to what many hard-line unionists or loyalists saw as Blair's appeasement of Irish republicans. In response to the flying of Israeli flags, Palestinian flags were flown in Catholic and nationalist neighbourhoods (Hill and White 2008). Though both Israeli and Palestinian flags had been displayed in the province before 2002, there was no precedent before then for the deployment of the symbols from a foreign conflict on such a scale in Northern Ireland, or perhaps anywhere.

Approaching a Definition

In his study, Nordlinger took a step-by-step approach to the definition of a deeply divided society. He acknowledged that all societies were differentiated along class or communal lines, or along both. Where people were conscious of such divisions and attached great importance to them and the segments took on a high degree of political salience, it was likely that conflict groups and organisations would emerge. But, according to Nordlinger, these only form the basis of a deeply divided society when the conflict is intense or severe. He then went on to discuss various ways in which the intensity of conflict might be measured. He concluded his discussion as follows:

> In short, a conflict is intense (or a society is deeply divided) when a large number of conflict group members attach overwhelming importance to the issues at stake, or manifest strongly held antagonistic beliefs and emotions towards the opposing segment, or both (Nordlinger 1972: 9).

He then identified violence and repression as possible consequences of this state of affairs.

But, while repression is clearly not an intrinsic aspect of the governance of a deeply divided society, there is a case for regarding violence as far more than simply a product or symptom of a deeply divided society. Violence and the threat of violence provide useful indicators of the intensity of antagonism between segments. Further, when violence and/or the threat of violence are persistent, the conditions are there for the creation of a long-term force field between the segments. Insofar as deeply divided societies are places where special measures of conflict regulation are needed, which was Nordlinger's point of departure for his study, what clearly matters is the connection between society's division and conflict beyond the level that might be found in a functioning liberal democracy. Thus, one way in which a deeply divided society might be distinguished from other societies is that in a deeply divided society conflict exists along a well-entrenched fault line that is recurrent and endemic and that contains the potential for violence between the segments.

An objection to the emphasis on the potential for violence as a defining characteristic of deeply divided societies is that episodic acts of collective violence occur in many societies that are not deeply divided. It might also be argued that the operation of conflict regulation mechanisms such as consociationalism can avert the possibility of violence. A difficulty in this context is that most successful examples of consociational democracy are to be found precisely in societies without a history of recurrent violence, prompting the jibe from critics of consociationalism that it only works where it is not needed. Responses to this line of argument have been, firstly, that it is in any event very difficult to achieve political stability in a deeply divided society and, secondly, that consociational mechanisms provide one of the few means for achieving political accommodation in such societies. These arguments are considered further in Chapter 7.

A further argument against treating the potential for widespread political violence as *the* basic distinguishing mark of a deeply divided society is that this condition is a sign of a more fundamental problem, that the polity is deficient in legitimacy. And an examination of a number of cases of deeply divided societies underscores the role of a contest over the legitimacy of the polity in entrenching division. For example, in the case of Northern Ireland, what has been in dispute between unionists and nationalists has been the legitimacy of the partition of Ireland. Unionists favour Northern Ireland's continued membership of the United Kingdom, while nationalists aspire to the creation of a united Ireland. One might see the origin of the Cyprus conflict in a somewhat similar light, with Greek Cypriots at the outset favouring *enosis* ('union') with Greece, while in response many Turkish Cypriots sought *taksim* ('partition'). Meron Benvenisti put forward the following striking description of the Israeli–Palestinian conflict in 1990:

> Both communities deny each other's standing as a legitimate entity. Hence, the Arabs define Zionism as racism – ergo illegitimate. The Israelis, in their turn, define Palestinian nationalism as PLO [Palestine Liberation Organisation] terrorism – ergo illegitimate. The delegitimisation is vital for both sides, for it enables them to believe in the exclusivity of their claim and in the absolute justice of their position (Benvenisti 1990: 123).

The Afrikaner nationalist blueprint for the future of South Africa under apartheid envisaged the country's transformation into at least 11 independent states. The ANC sought, in direct opposition to this project, one person one vote in an undivided country. One might similarly see the conflicts in the former Yugoslavia in the 1990s as arising out of the clash between the claims of secessionist nationalists for their own exclusive states and simultaneous projects for the creation of a Greater Serbia and a Greater Albania. Admittedly, this is to interpret the positions of the protagonists in these conflicts quite starkly and without reference to the narrative of justification in which such aims were embedded.

A feature of political debate within stable polities is that it takes place within the context of a wide measure of consensus on the framework for the making of decisions and an acceptance of the legitimacy of the outcomes of the political process. Deeply divided societies are characterised by just the opposite – a lack of consensus on the framework for the making of decisions and a contested political process in which the legitimacy of outcomes is commonly challenged by political representatives of one of the segments. These differences underscore why deeply divided societies should be so prone to violence. The forms that violence may take in such societies are examined in greater detail in Chapter 3.

It will have been noted from the examples discussed above that nationalism frequently plays a role in the contest for legitimacy in deeply divided societies. This is because nationalism provides a ready-made basis for the advancement of exclusivist claims on behalf of one or another segment. To be fair, nationalism can be couched in inclusive as well as exclusive terms, as the example of the non-racialism of the ANC shows. But the combination of ethnicity and nationalism in ethno-nationalism can be a powerfully destabilising force, as is illustrated by the rash of ethnic conflicts that followed the end of the Cold War.

The essence of ethno-nationalism is that the ethnic community should form the basis for the governance of independent states. It can be associated with majorities in existing states and to that extent does not necessarily challenge the territorial status quo. But ethno-nationalism also provides a strong basis for the claims of minorities to secession and for the creation of new states. Because territories are rarely ethnically homogeneous, the exclusivist tendencies of ethno-nationalism have a high propensity to generate conflict with those who do not belong to the ethnic community that is being mobilised behind the demand for ethnic self-determination. This topic, too, will be explored further below, primarily in Chapter 6.

3 VIOLENCE, ORDER AND JUSTICE

Concerns about violence are to be found in almost all societies. What is more specific to deeply divided societies is that political violence, or at least the threat of political violence, continually looms large in the concerns of its citizens. Security is not something that members of deeply divided societies are ever likely to take for granted. This chapter explores the reasons why. To approach this topic, it is advisable at the outset to get to grips with the concept of violence. While it might hardly be considered necessary to define the term, in fact the meaning of the word is more elusive than it might appear at first sight. In a thoughtful book on the subject, Gerald Priestland argued that 'the essence of violence is that physical power is deliberately employed with the ultimate sanction of physical pain and little choice but surrender or physical resistance' (Priestland 1974: 11). Two elements of his definition are worth underlining: Priestland's inclusion of intimidation within the scope of the term and the emphasis on intentions of the perpetrator of an act of violence. However, while Priestland's approach provides a useful basis for distinguishing the knife of the surgeon from that of the cut-throat, this does not entirely accord with common usage, since car crashes, particularly where they result in fatalities, are generally seen as violent events, although they are accidental in most cases.

A useful source both for the origins of terms and their usage are dictionaries. The second edition of the *Oxford English Dictionary* defines violence in the first instance as follows:

> the exercise of physical force so as to inflict injury on, or cause damage to, persons or property; action or conduct characterised by this; treatment or

usage tending to cause bodily injury or forcibly interfering with personal freedom. (Simpson and Weiner 1989: 654)

A curious feature of this definition is the inclusion of property but the exclusion of animals. This reflects the fact that many animals are reared with the explicit – and to most people acceptable – purpose of providing humans with food. However, attaching a firecracker to a cat's tail would be considered a violent act far beyond the ranks of the animal rights movement, just as it is easy to construct examples of damage to property – such as breaking a window to get into one's own house – that would not be seen as violent behaviour.

Force and Violence

The obvious difficulty in attempting to construct an objective definition of the term is that the word incorporates a very strong element of censure. Thus people tend to use the term 'violence' to indicate their disapproval of the behaviour in question. For this reason, a wide category of actions that would otherwise fit Priestland's definition quite well are usually excluded from common usage of the word, in particular the lawful actions of the authorities, including the judiciary, police, and army, in maintaining law and order and defending the country. The word typically used to distinguish such actions from violence is force. W. J. M. Mackenzie characterises this distinction as a word-play.

> Force–violence seem to be used as a 'we–they' pair, like 'we are patriotic they are jingo', 'we are reasonable they are fanatics', 'we are careful they are mean', and so on. 'We' use force, 'they' use violence. A Rugby correspondent paying tribute to a pack of forwards might call them 'rugged' or 'vigorous' or even 'forceful'. But to say 'violent' would be to say that they go beyond the limit of the rules as 'we' understand them. Violence is dangerous play. (Mackenzie 1975: 120)

In a stable society characterised by a large measure of consensus, the realms of force and violence often appear to be readily separable because of their very different connotations. Thus, force tends to be associated with actions that are legal, legitimate, controlled, regulated, reactive, institutionalised, impersonal, defensive and directed at upholding the existing order, while violence, by contrast, tends to be associated with actions that are illegal, illegitimate, uncontrolled, arbitrary, unpredictable, spontaneous, emotional, aggressive and a threat to the existing order, whether actually so intended or not. Of these pairings, the most critical is the legitimate–illegitimate pairing, so that legitimate violence is virtually a synonym for force, as is evident in the formulation that the state possesses a monopoly of legitimate violence.

Of course, how the institutions for the maintenance of law and order are viewed in a society has a very large bearing on their functioning. Thus in a society in which the authorities are seen almost universally as legitimate it is possible for the law to be enforced effectively by a police force that uses a minimum degree of physical coercion in the vast majority of cases. This is because police officers will be able to rely on the co-operation of most members of society and their authority will rarely be challenged when they need to use it to compel obedience. The very fact that the authorities are usually able to maintain order effectively without violating the rights of members of the society or, to put it more simply, without routinely meting out rough treatment to possible suspects and witnesses tends to reinforce their legitimacy. By contrast, in any situation where the authorities are not seen as legitimate by a section of society, it is very difficult for the law to be enforced, except with resort to physical coercion. Further, association of the maintenance of law and order with such actions tends to reinforce its lack of legitimacy from the perspective of those on the receiving end of such treatment or who feel threatened by it.

In a relatively homogeneous or moderately divided society, security can be provided through what can conveniently be labelled the rule-of-law model for maintaining order. This provides a mechanism for the criminalisation of violence, as that term is understood by most members of the society. It comprises judicial authority, standing above society and employing the resources of the state to enforce its judgements, which are directed against individuals. Thus, for the purpose of judicial authority, society consists of individuals and, if any individual transgresses the rules of society, he or she is punished. Thus, in the simple case of A attacking B, the state takes action against A through the criminal justice system and that is the end of the matter. In reality, society may be faced with a victim B, but difficulty in establishing the identity of A. The system has to be sufficiently reliable in punishing the guilty without transgressing the rights of innocent people if it is to retain general public confidence.

Also important to the functioning of the rule-of-law model is the principle of equality before the law. Precisely because no society is composed of a set of equal individuals, this principle is often not universally upheld in practice. The rich and the well-connected generally fare better than the poor and/or those from groups with a low status in the society in question. In the case of both the United States and mainland Britain, racial minorities have consistently been badly treated by the criminal justice system. The Rodney King case in the United States and the Stephen Lawrence case in Britain highlighted the persistence of the problem in the 1990s, despite the outward political consensus, in both societies, that people should be treated equally before the law regardless of race. However, for the most part, in moderately divided societies cross-cutting cleavages of one kind or another tend to limit the influence of group loyalties upon the functioning of the criminal justice system sufficiently for the rule-of-law model to retain its general credibility.

A caveat has now to be added to this argument as a result of developments in the first decade of the twenty-first century. Mass casualty terrorism, epitomised by the events of 9/11 in the United States and of 7/7 in Britain, has resulted in significant departures from the rule-of-law model in relation to the threat of international terrorism, most specifically from the network of global jihadists known as al Qaeda. Extraordinary measures have been adopted in both the United States and Britain to address the issue, which run counter to basic precepts, for instance that individuals should not be detained for long periods in the absence of criminal proceedings against them. The authoritarianism of the Blair government in Britain and of the Bush administration in the United States damaged the rule of law in both societies and its legacy remains largely intact, despite changes of government in both countries. In Britain's case, the Blair government perversely failed to pay heed to the country's own recent experience from Northern Ireland, of how not to respond to terrorism (English 2009: 127–8). However, many other Western democracies that have not faced the same level of threat have remained committed to the rule-of-law model when dealing with terrorism.

In a book comparing the approaches of a number of countries to combating terrorism, James Beckman emphasised that the United States was, relatively speaking, new to the field of protecting the homeland from the threat of terrorism. Beckman noted that in the wake of 9/11 the United States adopted a two-fold approach of strengthening domestic laws and of taking military action abroad to pre-empt the threat of further attacks on American soil. A candid explanation of his rationale for the launch of the global war on terror after 9/11 was given by President Bush in his 2004 State of the Union address:

> I know that some people question if America is really in a war at all. They view terrorism more as a crime, a problem to be solved mainly with law enforcement and indictments. After the World Trade Center was first attacked in 1993, some of the guilty were indicted and tried and convicted, and sent to prison. But the matter was not settled. The terrorists were still training

and plotting in other nations, and drawing up more ambitious plans. After the chaos and carnage of September 11th, it is not enough to serve our enemies with legal papers. The terrorists and their supporters declared war on the United States, and war is what they got. (Quoted in Beckman 2007: 163–4)

But, while some countries responded to the threat posed by the mass casualty terrorism practised by al Qaeda through special measures that suspend the normal rights that defendants are accorded in ordinary criminal cases, even those involving the most serious offences, there has simultaneously been an extension of the law to address issues that would previously have been seen as lying outside the remit of the legal process. International tribunals were set up to provide a legal framework for the prosecution of crimes committed in the course of the wars in the Balkans in the 1990s and during the genocide in Rwanda in 1994. Further, an international criminal court has been established for the purpose of making it possible to bring to book political leaders who commit acts of genocide, perpetrate war crimes or carry out other gross violations of human rights. But a major weakness of this framework is that it cannot possibly offer the prospect of equality before the law, given the huge disparities in power among states. Hitherto the focus of the court and of prosecutors has largely been on political leaders in relatively weak African states. There is also a substantial danger of the associated notions of 'no immunity' and 'no impunity' providing an obstacle to political accommodation in countries seeking a negotiated way out of violent conflict. In deeply divided societies, righteous anger over the crimes committed by, or on behalf of, the other community presents a difficulty for the initiation, let alone the success, of negotiations across communal divisions. Amnesties commonly form an element in negotiated settlements to end long-running conflicts. They are now threatened by the new legal norms (Hadden 2004).

Dominant and Subordinate Communities

In Chapter 1 two broad types of deeply divided societies were identified: societies horizontally divided between a dominant and a subordinate community and societies vertically divided. The distinction is important in this context, since whether a society is horizontally or vertically divided tends to give rise to different patterns of violence. The former case will be considered first. Where a society is polarised between a dominant and a subordinate community, an individual's membership of one or the other is a matter of critical importance in how he or she is treated. In a society deeply divided between a dominant and a subordinate community, the simple case of A attacking B typically produces four different possibilities, which give rise to four very different outcomes. If A and B are both members of the dominant community, then something approximating to the process of justice under the rule-of-law model is likely, with A being criminalised as an individual. If A and B are both members of the subordinate community, then the most likely response of the authorities is one of indifference, since servicing the needs of the subordinate community tends to have a low priority.

In the case that A, the perpetrator, comes from the dominant community and B, the victim, is from the subordinate community, the bias of the criminal justice system towards the dominant community will operate in favour of the accused, should matters even reach that point. Almost regardless of the precise circumstances of the case, the accused can expect lenient treatment. This is because it will be judged not in the context of the interaction of individuals but in the light of the dominant community's fear of resistance by the subordinate community to its status. Any evidence that B was behaving in a provocative manner from the standpoint of members of the dominant community will usually be sufficient to ensure A's acquittal. By contrast, if A, the perpetrator, is a member of the subordinate community and B, the victim, a member of the dominant community, the accused can expect to be extremely severely punished. Every dominant community's nightmare is that its most vulnerable members will be physically assaulted by members of the subordinate community, and when such instances occur there is invariably a call for exemplary punishment, both to assert the dominant community's power and to deter further attacks.

Apartheid South Africa abounded in examples of differential justice in the four ways described above. The relative indifference of the authorities to crime in the townships explains one of the paradoxes of the apartheid era, namely that South Africa had a relatively small police force in relation to its population, notwithstanding the image of the country as a police state (Cawthra 1993: 4). The townships under apartheid proved a breeding ground for vigilantism of various kinds precisely because of the ineffectiveness of state efforts to combat crime. The priorities of the police were to protect the white suburbs against crime and to safeguard the state against political subversion. Under white minority rule, punishment in rape cases was particularly severe, commonly involving the death penalty when the race of the perpetrator was black and the victim white. Thus, in the years 1911 to 1968, only two of those executed for the crime of rape were white, out of a total of 132, and in both cases the victims were also white. The disparity in sentences occasionally caused controversy – as when a newspaper reported that a coloured man had been sentenced to death for the rape of a white woman aged 52, while a white man who had raped a 9-year-old Indian girl had been sentenced to nine months in prison (Sachs 1973: 155).

As Sachs notes after discussing judicial attitudes to race in the case of rape, '[t]he figures for murder across the colour line present a similar picture of leniency towards whites and severity towards blacks' (ibid.). An African killing an animal in a game park for food could expect punishment as severe as that of a white farmer found guilty of the manslaughter of an African farm worker, the punishment being a substantial fine in each case. The operation of the criminal justice system under apartheid has been savagely satirised by Tom Sharpe. In his novel *Riotous Assembly*, a police constable is confronted with an unsolicited and unwelcome confession by a wealthy white spinster, Miss Hazelstone, that she had murdered her Zulu cook. Her futile efforts to be arrested occur at the start of the novel and form a running theme of the book (Sharpe 1973: 16).

These attitudes can also be found in societies that are not deeply divided but in which there is strong prejudice against a racial, religious or ethnic minority, and they affect the operation of the justice system in a similar way. Between 1995 and 2000 in the United States, blacks and Hispanics were defendants in 72 per cent of cases in which the death penalty was sought by prosecutors. While there were roughly equal numbers of whites and blacks and Hispanics charged with murder, white murderers were far more likely to be offered plea bargains. Even more strikingly, the death penalty was twice as likely to be sought in the case of a black defendant when the victim was white (*Federal Death Penalty System* 2000). The issue of general racial bias was addressed in 1987 in a case before the Supreme Court, which narrowly rejected, by five votes to four, this bias as a reason for treating the operation of the penalty as tainted (Dow 2011). The war on drugs provides another area in which disparity of treatment between the races in the United States remains evident. Thus Martin Wolf noted, in an article discussing the 2011 report of the Global Commission on Drug Policy: 'Though African Americans are just 14 per cent of regular drug users, they account for 37 per cent of drug arrests and 56 per cent of those in prison' (Wolf 2011). Admittedly, racial bias may not be entirely responsible for these stark global disparities. Other factors, in themselves not directly related to race, may also be affecting the figures and would be evident on a more fine-tuned examination of the evidence. But the likelihood that other factors could explain away the disparities altogether is highly improbable.

The unequal enforcement of the law provides one of the principal means by which a dominant community maintains its hegemony over a subordinate community in a deeply divided society. As long as the dominant community is able to maintain its hegemony, such societies may appear orderly as well as politically stable, even to the outside observer. Indeed, dominant communities frequently associate the condition of peace with acquiescence on the part of the subordinate community in its inferior social position. Thus the initial reaction of members of the dominant community to challenges from below is frequently a desire to restore tranquillity by putting members of the subordinate community back in their place. Reform in these circumstances is fraught with difficulty. In particular, if, in the context of attempting to establish the principle of equality before the law, the legal authorities are perceived as failing to punish sufficiently severely violent acts committed by members of the subordinate community and directed at those above them, there is always the danger that some members of the dominant community will take the law into their own hands. In circumstances of a changing balance of power between the communities, such reactions may set off cycles of retaliation between the communities.

Representative Violence

Frank Wright coined the expression 'representative violence' to describe violence in situations in which the victims of violence are perceived as being chosen not because of their individual characteristics but because they are identified as representing a certain group of people. He spelt out the implications of such perceptions as follows:

> This condition of representative violence is very simple. If anyone of a great number of people can be 'punished' for something done by the community they come from, and if the communities are sufficiently clearly defined, there is a risk that anyone attacking a member of the other community can set in motion an endless chain of violence. Even if few aspects of the representative violence enjoy widespread support of the kind that could be established by opinion polls, it is only necessary for people to *understand* what is happening for it to create a generalised danger. Everyone might be a target for reprisal for something done in their name and without their approval. To break up representative violence, an authority had to be able to pursue all people engaged in violence and to criminalise them without any challenges to its authority. But if long-established relationships of violence exist, the law has to be able to obliterate all pleas of mitigating circumstance which the cycle of violence throws up. It cannot for example accept as defence for actions that they are 'deterrence actions', 'pre-emptive strikes', 'anticipatory self-defence', or 'reprisals', even if these correspond

to people's actual experiences and perceptions of things. If the law does accept such pleas, it cannot function. And if its capacity to function is impaired, then the only kind of tranquillity that there can ever be is a form of truce or stable pattern of communal deterrence. The law becomes only a balancing wheel in this system. It is not the source of tranquillity. (Wright 1987: 11–2)

Societies that are divided vertically rather than horizontally may also be prone to the creation of cycles of violence and the institutionalisation of representative violence. The effects of conflict among vertically segmented groups can be just as devastating as those that arise from the breakdown of a dominant group's hegemony, as the case of the former Yugoslavia demonstrates, where no single community occupied a dominant position during the years of communist rule. Indeed, the strength of ethno-nationalism in each ethnic group was a reflection of a perception common to all of Yugoslavia's nationalities that members of their group had been disadvantaged in one way or another under communism.

Subordination of all indigenous communities under colonial rule also tends to produce vertical lines of division in former colonies. Even when one group is much larger than the other, as in the conflict between Greeks and Turks in Cyprus or in that between Sinhalese and Tamils in Sri Lanka, the larger ethnic group does not see itself as, nor does it constitute in practice, a dominant group. In fact a dominant group may be a minority of the population, as the example of South Africa under apartheid demonstrates. In the case of both Northern Ireland and Israel/Palestine, the dominant community has constituted a majority of the population, though in both these instances a factor contributing to the fearful, siege mentality of the dominant community is the perception that it is a minority within a wider framework – that of the island in the case of Northern Ireland Protestants and that of the Middle East as a region in the case of Israeli Jews.

Consequences of a Lack of Consensus

As was argued in Chapter 2, deeply divided societies are characterised by a lack of consensus on the framework for the making of decisions and by a contested political process in which the legitimacy of its outcomes is challenged by one segment of the society. In the case of a vertically divided society, the strategy of the disaffected community (or communities) is likely to be directed primarily at exit from the polity through secession, partition or union with another state. In the case of horizontally segmented societies, the issue of equality among the communities looms larger, as a

priority of the subordinate community. Northern Ireland provides an inter-
esting instance, in which the subordinate community maintains an aspiration to a united Ireland but in which its political representatives have been
willing to accept arrangements guaranteeing its equality within the existing
contested boundaries as the basis of an historic compromise with the
dominant community. Ironically, it has been the dominant community that
has been the more reluctant to accept the settlement contained in the
Belfast Agreement, even though it involves acceptance of partition until/
unless there is a majority vote in favour of a united Ireland.

A common characteristic of a horizontally deeply divided society is that
the state's monopoly of legitimate violence is contested by the subordinate
community. At best, members of a subordinate community may acquiesce
in the operation of the state's institutions on the grounds of their community's powerlessness. But, just as importantly, the dominant community,
too, in such situations often has an attitude towards questions of force and
violence that is different from those to be found in societies in which there
is a consensus on these issues. This stems from the dominant community's
perception of the existence of a serious challenge to the legitimacy of
the state from the subordinate community. Rosenbaum and Sederberg
use the terms 'establishment violence' and 'vigilantism' (Rosenbaum and
Sederberg 1976: 4–29) to describe pro-status quo violence that differs
from force or legitimate violence because it openly runs counter to the law.
Their book is entitled *Vigilante Politics*, and in fact vigilantism is a better
term of the two for the phenomena they describe. What is characteristic of
vigilantes is their distrust of the process of maintaining order through the
criminalisation of individual perpetrators after a fair trial in court.

Vigilantes appear from time to time in politically stable liberal democracies, when the criminal justice system appears ineffective in dealing with
ordinary crime. The Guardian Angels, an organisation formed in 1979 in
reaction to the high crime rate in New York, provides one example. The
activities of the Guardian Angels included patrolling the New York subway.
Volunteers wore red berets, to signal their presence to the general public,
and they were trained to carry out citizen's arrests. Their actions proved
controversial and on occasion led to conflict with the police (Hays 1988).
In deeply divided societies, fighting crime may nominally be a justification
for the activities of vigilantes, but their real and often openly declared
aim is to quell the political assertiveness of the subordinate community.
In any event, it is a feature of deeply divided societies that maintaining
order, including combating crime, tends to be seen as synonymous
with keeping members of the subordinate community in their place. The
greater the perceived threat from the subordinate community, the more
aggressively violent vigilantes from the dominant community tend to

be. At the height of Northern Ireland's troubles, loyalist paramilitary organisations engaged in a campaign of random sectarian assassinations. A widely used slogan was: 'Any Catholic will do'. Members of the Afrikaner Weerstandsbeweging (AWB – Afrikaner resistance movement) in South Africa were responsible for a number of random attacks on African civilians in the period leading up to and including the country's first democratic elections. But by far the best known of the white supremacist vigilante organisations is the American Ku Klux Klan. The Klan was active in a number of periods. It was originally formed by veterans of the American Civil War in the 1860s, but it was at its most influential in the period between the First and the Second World Wars, when its membership ran into the millions. A third period when the Klan was active was the 1950s and 1960s, when it was associated with violent resistance to civil rights, particularly in the Deep South. However, the Klan's role in opposing the progress of the civil rights movement was secondary to the obstacles the movement faced from Southern politicians, officials and law enforcement officers.

Communal Deterrence

Vigilantism is the most extreme form of a much larger pattern of behaviour by members of dominant communities in deeply divided societies that is encapsulated in Frank Wright's term 'communal deterrence'. One such mechanism, historically, was segregation, which was not just an assertion of racial prejudice, or even primarily intended to satisfy atavistic attitudes in the dominant community. Rather its chief purpose was to disempower the subordinate community through denying its members access to the full resources of the society. One of the milder forms of communal deterrence is constituted by the parades of the Orange Order in Northern Ireland. Originally these parades were a way in which Protestants asserted their dominance over Catholics in the whole of the north-east of Ireland, by marches that purposively went through Catholic areas. While the marches were ritualistic displays of aggression, they served the purpose of uniting Protestants and underlining sectarian divisions. However, their primary objective was to remind Catholics of their subordinate position in society. The fear behind this objective was encapsulated in the Orange song, which called on 'Croppies' to 'lie down'. 'Croppies' is a colloquial expression for 'Catholics', derived from the rebellion of 1798, when the rebels earned this nickname because of the way they cut their hair. The parades of the Orange Order are still a cause of civil disturbance in Northern Ireland, though these days they only pass through Catholic areas in a relatively small number of instances. Controversy over the routes of Orange marches was a cause of widespread rioting in Northern Ireland in the summers of 1995, 1996, 1997 and 1998. And, despite the political settlement embodied in the 1998 Belfast Agreement, the issue led to localised rioting in September 2005, and again in July 2010, on a scale that attracted international media coverage and raised doubts about the success of the peace process.

Metropolitan authorities (whether one is referring to the federal government of the United States in relation to the Deep South, the government in London in relation to Northern Ireland or the case of an imperial centre in relation to the activities of settlers in the periphery) generally do not like mechanisms of communal deterrence. For example, this is brought out lucidly in Wright's own detailed account of Ulster politics before the 1880s (Wright 1996). The explanation is that the authorities rightly see such mechanisms as obstacles to the eventual integration of members of the subordinate community as full and equal citizens of the polity and to the establishment of the rule-of-law model of ordering society. Institutions associated with communal deterrence are also an obstacle to efforts of reformers when the hegemony of the dominant community can no longer be sustained for demographic or other reasons. But, even when the mechanisms of communal deterrence themselves are dismantled, the mentality that underpins them may survive, as illustrated by the penal policies of the Southern states of the United States, particularly the political support, within the white community, for capital punishment. In fact the siege mentality of dominant or formerly dominant communities often remains remarkably persistent even after radical political change has taken place.

The political representatives of subordinate communities usually emphasise that their goal is equality of status between members of different communities rather than a reversal of roles in which the formerly subordinate community becomes the dominant community and vice versa. Of course, in practice, if the subordinate community outnumbers the dominant community, the effect of equality is that the representatives of the former will wield most political power. That may be balanced by the continuing influence of the dominant community in other fields, particularly the economic. Partly for that reason, even if the ideology of the new ruling party rejects the old lines of division in society, the subordinate community's experience of discrimination and of being on the receiving end of aggressive coercion by the dominant community in the past is likely to colour its attitude in the new situation. The point can be illustrated by the extent of racial polarisation over the workings of the criminal justice system in post-apartheid South Africa. An example is the furore created by the Nicholas Steyn case.

Steyn was convicted in 1999 of the culpable homicide of a 6-month-old baby, Angelina Zwane, and sentenced to five years of imprisonment, three of them suspended. The circumstances of the baby's death were that Steyn had fired three shots when a 12-year-old carrying her baby cousin on her back had crossed Steyn's smallholding near Benoni on 11 April 1998. The night before the property had come under attack from armed robbers and Steyn's response was due to his fear of a repetition of that attack. The shots that Steyn fired were evidently intended as warning shots, but one of them had struck an overhead electricity cable and the ricochet killed the baby. This last piece of information emerged at the trial and resulted in the dropping of a charge of murder against Steyn. Prior to the trial the tragic death of Angelina Zwane had attracted huge publicity, as proof that the attitude of some whites remained unchanged from the era of apartheid and, most unforgivably, that they continued to regard African lives as of little account. The outcome of the trial divided the country, with an editorial in one newspaper arguing that Steyn should have been acquitted. However, the predominant reaction was outrage at the leniency of the sentence. Among those who expressed disquiet at the sentence on this score was the minister of justice, Dullah Omar (van Schalkwyk 1999: 5–7).

Inter-communal violence creates force fields, the effects of which can be very long-lasting. Violence in the Balkans during the 1990s owed much to the revival of force fields created during the Second World War. In particular, memory of the mass killings of Serbs in Croatian concentration camps in the 1940s was a major influence on Serbian resistance to the redrawing of boundaries in the Balkans that left Serbs as minorities in a number of independent states dominated by other ethnic groups. However, from the perspective of other ethnic groups, the blame for conflict lay with the aggressive attempt of Serbs led by Milošević to carve a Greater Serbia out of the breakup of Yugoslavia. In reality, these are, simply, different sides of the same coin. This is not to underestimate the importance of how the onset of violence is interpreted. Perceptions of who threw the first stone may have a profound bearing on external views of the legitimacy of contending parties in a conflict. As Mackenzie puts it somewhat cynically, 'it is prudent to entrap the other side into violence if there is in fact a watching public which is capable of reacting against those who break the rules' (Mackenzie 1975: 121).

The language used to justify violence or force provides a strong indication of the existence of a force field. Terms commonly used in the context of inter-communal conflicts include retaliation, deterrence, pre-emptive strikes, holding the line, clearing the decks, collective punishment, tit for tat, exemplary actions, exacting a price, reprisal. The terminology is similar to that used by states in the context of war. It is also worth noting that the language used when the killing stops also tends to follow that of war, so there is a ceasefire, a truce, a cessation, a pause or a suspension of hostilities. The image is of two armies facing each other and ready to re-engage. Unfortunately, that may not be far from the mark. In the context of Lebanon's civil war between 1975 and 1992, there were more than a hundred ceasefires, some of which broke down within hours of coming into effect. When a society has been magnetised by the existence of a force field, a single incident can trigger a cycle of violence that can threaten to plunge the society into an abyss. The level of tension in a society may remain very high even when the actual incidence of violence is relatively low, so widespread is the fear of the possibility of escalation, and even of civil war. Such fears were commonly expressed during Northern Ireland's troubles between 1968 and 1994, even when the numbers being killed each year had fallen below a hundred.

The level of antagonism between the segments in a deeply divided society is reflected in the attention that the segments attach to their relative power. Demography is an obsession in deeply divided societies, since the relative size of each of the segments is commonly seen as having implications for the balance of power between them. And this is a rational assumption insofar as the outcome of elections in deeply divided societies is widely understood to hinge on each segment's share of the adult population. This is reflected in the importance the segments pay to such issues as immigration and birth rates because of their potential to alter the proportion of the population belonging to one segment or the other. But the size of the segments may also be affected by violence. And indeed a dominant segment or community may deliberately seek the elimination of the other segment or community, conceivably through a policy of genocide. Alternatively and more plausibly, it might seek the same result of eliminating the others through a programme designed to remove them from the society by forcible means. This approach has been encapsulated in the term 'ethnic cleansing', which entered the English language from Serbo-Croat as a result of events in the Balkans in the early 1990s.

Genocide and Ethnic Cleansing

Both genocide and ethnic cleansing deserve further examination in the context of deeply divided societies. But it needs to be stated at the outset that the relationship between these concepts and violence within deeply divided societies is far from straightforward. Genocide represents the most extreme response imaginable to diversity: the killing of members of a group with the objective of their total elimination from a society. The term was coined by Raphael Lemkin, in a book entitled *Axis Rule in Occupied Europe*, published in 1944. He described genocide as 'directed against the national group as an entity', so that 'the actions involved are directed against the individuals, not in their individual capacity, but as members of the national group' (Lemkin 1944: 79). The obvious context of Lemkin's invention of this new word was the Holocaust – the Nazi extermination of the Jews – and its timeliness was reflected in its rapid acceptance into common usage.

In 1946 the United Nations General Assembly passed a resolution declaring genocide to be a crime under international law, and that was followed by the 1948 United Nations Convention on the Prevention and Punishment of the Crime of Genocide. The Convention approached the issue of definition as follows:

> In the present Convention, genocide means any of the following acts committed with intent to destroy, in whole or in part, a national, ethnical, racial or religious group, as such:
>
> (a) killing members of the group;
> (b) causing serious bodily or mental harm to members of the group;
> (c) deliberately inflicting on the group conditions of life calculated to bring about its physical destruction in whole or in part;
> (d) imposing measures intended to prevent births within the group;
> (e) forcibly transferring children of the group to another group. (Quoted in Kuper 1981: 210–14)

This definition can be compared with the far simpler definition of the *Concise Oxford English Dictionary* – 'the mass extermination of human beings, especially of a particular race or nation' (Thompson 1995: 565).

In one sense the Convention definition is very broad, including other ways of destroying a group than the killing of its members – which provides a logical basis for the argument that events such as the Irish potato famine of the nineteenth century constitute genocide. In fact, on this basis, all famines that bear heavily on a particular group might be so categorised, on the grounds that famines invariably involve human agency and not simply an absolute shortage of food. But is it reasonable to label events that do not involve mass murder as genocide? Treating the means listed in (b) to (e) above as additional to direct killings would avoid the implication that it is possible for there to be a genocide without the deliberate killing of anyone. At the same time, the Convention definition does not encompass, as the dictionary definition does, the mass murder of political opponents or the elimination of classes of people such as the intelligentsia or the kulaks killed by Stalin. A practical consequence of this limitation is that members of the international community have managed to evade their responsibilities under the Convention by arguing, as in the case of Rwanda in 1994, that, because the Hutu militia killed moderate Hutu politicians as well as Tutsis in general, this example of mass killings fell outside the scope of the Convention. When President Clinton visited Rwanda in March 1998, he touched on this issue briefly, accepting: 'We did not act quickly enough [. . .] We did not immediately call these crimes by their rightful name, genocide' (Ryle 1998).

However, the avoidance of the term 'genocide' by states not wishing to take action under the Genocide Convention has been overtaken by a different problem: the widespread use of the term to cover practically any case of mass killing, so as to provide a justification for Western intervention. The effect has been to dilute the force of both the word and the Convention. And there remains considerable contention, for example, over whether the use of the term is appropriate in the case of Darfur. However, there remains broad agreement that three sets of events stand out as clear-cut cases of genocide in the twentieth century: the Armenian genocide during the First World War, when 1.5 million Armenians out of a population of 2 million in the Ottoman Empire were killed; the Holocaust, that is, the killing of 6 million Jews by the Nazis in the period 1933 to 1945, but primarily in the final solution phase between 1941 and 1945; and the killing of 800,000 Tutsis in Rwanda between April and July 1994 (Destexhe 1994–5). The case of the Herero of German South West Africa at the beginning of the century might legitimately be added on the basis of the intent of the perpetrators. The reason this case is commonly excluded is the much smaller scale of the killings. By contrast, the huge scale of the killings in Cambodia in Year Zero is a reason why this case is sometimes included as an example of genocide, though the motive for the killings and the identity of the perpetrators make its inclusion within the category of genocide problematic.

From a comparative study of the three clear cases of genocide it is possible to identify a number of factors that, in combination, are associated with the extreme circumstances in which genocide may occur. These include a dominant community made insecure by a series of disasters; a situation in which war and the isolation it brings remove constraints on the dominant community's use of violence; a vulnerable target group that falls outside the universe of moral obligation of the dominant community; and external threats beyond the capacity of the dominant community to overcome (Fein 1990: 71–5). Of course, Fein did not anticipate the killings in Rwanda, but it is striking that her criteria, drawn from the earlier two cases, fit the Rwanda case as well. Perception of the target group as disloyal, whether or not it is actually connected to the external threats the dominant community faces, has been a significant factor in many cases. However, it is important to emphasise the subjective basis of many of the factors that contribute to the dominant community's insecurity. And the argument might be made that regimes in the grip of a racist ideology fall into a different category from governments with a disposition to distrust minorities with transnational links to neighbouring states.

In their analysis of genocide, Chalk and Jonassohn stress the role that government plays in creating the conditions for genocide.

> [I]n order to perform a genocide the perpetrator has always had to first organize a campaign that redefined the victim group as worthless, outside the web of mutual obligations, a threat to the people, immoral sinners and/or sub-humans. Even after such a campaign of vilification and dehumanization the actual performance of the mass killings seems to have required a good deal of coercion and centralized control [. . .] it seems that mass killing is extremely difficult for ordinary people to carry out; it requires the recruitment of pathological individuals and criminals. (Chalk and Jonassohn 1990: 28)

However, this view has been challenged, most strongly by Daniel Goldhagen in *Hitler's Willing Executioners: Ordinary Germans and the Holocaust*.

> To the very end, the ordinary Germans who perpetrated the Holocaust wilfully, faithfully, and zealously slaughtered Jews. They did so even when they were risking their own capture. They did so even when they received a command from no less a personage than Himmler that they desist their killings. (Goldhagen 1997: 371)

The way in which genocide occurred in Rwanda under a government incapable of defending its territory provides further support for this argument (Prunier 1995). It must be acknowledged that Goldhagen is a controversial scholar and that aspects of his writings have come in for a lot of criticism from historians, especially his positing of a pervasive anti-Semitism peculiar to Germany to underpin his empirical analysis. However, the central point being emphasised here has also been made by others whose scholarship is not in question, most notably by Christopher Browning in his path-breaking study of the role of a reserve police battalion in mass killings in Poland (Browning 2001).

Chalk and Jonassohn make one other point that is very relevant to the issue of the possibility of genocide in a deeply divided society. They argue that one of the defining characteristics of genocide is its one-sided nature. This seems a plausible proposition, since genocide would hardly seem to be feasible without the existence of a very large measure of inequality in the power of the perpetrators and that of the victims. And the pursuit of the objective of physical elimination of any group would seem to presuppose that the group in question lacks any immediate means of self-defence. These are not conditions that are commonly to be found in a deeply divided society, since one of its key characteristics, as previously discussed, is that there is a contest and a conflict over the legitimacy of the existing polity. That implies that, even in a horizontally divided society, the subordinate community is not utterly powerless. Chalk and Jonassohn's point fits the cases of the Armenian genocide and of the Holocaust; but then neither Nazi Germany nor Turkey under the Committee of Union and Progress is commonly thought of as a deeply divided society, given the political marginality of the minorities targeted by these regimes. However, both Rwanda and Burundi have been widely characterised as deeply divided societies. And the history of genocide and mass killings in the two societies is clearly connected, with successive episodes of mass killing of Hutus in Burundi under regimes dominated by Tutsis providing part of the inspiration for the Hutu *génocidaires* in Rwanda.

Further, the attitude that the very existence of the other community constitutes a threat to one's own is quite commonly to be found in deeply divided societies. Indeed it helps to explain the ferocity of civil wars in such societies. A dominant community may go to extraordinary lengths to find ways of reducing the numbers and power of a subordinate community that threatens its hold over the society. An example is the chemical and biological weapons programme instituted during the crisis years of apartheid in South Africa. Among the schemes that the head of Project Coast, Wouter Basson, dreamt up in the quest to prolong the existence of apartheid was research aiming to discover a race-specific bacterial agent that could be used to sterilise the country's black population (Finnegan 2001). But, generally speaking, expulsion is a more feasible objective than preventing a group's reproduction as a way of altering the balance of power in a deeply divided society. In the case of Israel, the policy proposal of seeking the forcible removal of Palestinians from the polity is euphemistically referred to as transfer and has support on the radical right of Israeli opinion. Historians such as Benny Morris have established that one of the main objectives of Israeli forces during the country's war of independence was to reduce the size of the Arab population in the process and that this entailed the widespread use of coercion to induce the flight of Palestinians from the country (Morris 1987).

In its most extreme form – that of the ethnic cleansing practised in the Balkans during the 1990s – expulsion may be accompanied by mass killings. However, this is a means to achieving the more limited objective of removing members of a group from a particular area. And whether that is achieved on a temporary or on a permanent basis may depend on local and shifting power balances. As the case of the former Yugoslavia during the 1990s demonstrated, yesterday's perpetrator of ethnic cleansing may be tomorrow's victim, and vice versa. Such cycles of violence are all too characteristic of deeply divided societies. Part of their dynamic is intense levels of collective insecurity, which support assumptions of 'cleanse or be cleansed'. But mass killings may occur for reasons other than the desire to annihilate a group or to drive it out of a territory. The commonest is to compel obedience to a central government that large numbers of people in the affected area or region regard as illegitimate. In extreme cases, this may result in killings on a scale that matches cases of genocide. An example is provided by the mass killings that followed Indonesia's occupation of East Timor in 1975.

The unique disapprobation that is attached by the international community to the crime of genocide explains why there is a tendency to label mass killings, whatever their purpose, as 'genocide', especially if the killings are on a very large scale. Thus, those seeking the punishment of the perpetrators of mass killings argue that a broad interpretation of the concept of genocide is necessary to ensure that such perpetrators do not escape justice. And this view has become predominant, insofar as those who have come to dominate the debate on what to do about mass killings and other crimes against humanity are lawyers concerned with justice and influenced by the assumption that events such as mass killings are the product of evil intentions of a few rather than of structural conditions obtaining in a particular socio-economic and political context. However, from an analytical perspective, differences in motivation are significant.

Whether the objective of a government's policy is the elimination of a group, its expulsion, or merely its political repression does matter. In this context, it is worth underlining that unambiguous cases of genocide are relatively rare, while the use of coercion by governments to compel obedience is widespread. And miscalculations in this context, by a government or by its opponents, can lead to slaughter on a large scale. The belief that the very selective punishment of some of the perpetrators of such violence represents a sensible way to tackle this problem seems naïve at best. Its widespread promulgation under the misleading, if not hypocritical, slogan of 'no impunity' must be counted as another obstacle to peacemaking in deeply divided societies, since a critical task in any deeply divided society is to overcome the self-righteousness that identifies the interests of one community with justice, to the exclusion of the claims of others.

The Deadly Ethnic Riot

The focus on genocide has tended to deflect the world's attention from lesser but far more prevalent forms of lethal violence, which afflict many societies and play a significant role in both generating and entrenching social divisions. The most important of these from the perspective of this book – though it is by no means confined to deeply divided societies – is the deadly ethnic riot. It is the subject of a monumental study by Donald Horowitz. He defines it as follows:

> A deadly ethnic riot is an intense, sudden, though not necessarily wholly unplanned, lethal attack by civilian members of one ethnic group on civilian members of another ethnic group, the victims chosen because of their group membership. (Horowitz 2001: 1)

In this context, 'ethnic' should be interpreted to encompass the variety of communal divisions discussed in Chapter 2. A few examples of deadly ethnic riots from 2009, 2010 and 2011 will serve to underline the contemporary relevance of the phenomenon. In July 2009 Uighurs and Han Chinese clashed in the Xinjiang region of China, with a death toll of at least 156 (Soares 2009). The riots followed in the wake of a confrontation between the police and a demonstration demanding that the authorities investigate the deaths of two Uighur migrant workers in a brawl. As many as 2,000 people were estimated to have died in June 2010 in ethnic warfare in Kyrgyzstan between Kyrgyz and Uzbek residents following the ouster of the country's President (Harding 2010). On a smaller scale, there were 15 deaths and 242 people injured in clashes between Muslims and Copts in Egypt in May 2011 (Cockburn 2011). The violence occurred after Muslims laid siege to a church where they believed a convert to Islam was being held. As these examples underline, the circumstances in which deadly ethnic violence occurs vary widely. They happen under all types of regime, though it is worth noting that two of the cases coincided with political transitions.

Some societies do appear especially susceptible to the deadly ethnic riot. The outstanding modern example is India. There have been numerous deadly riots between Hindus and Muslims since the country's independence. Their prevalence, as well as lethality, has been the subject of intensive study. An important work on the issue is Ashutosh Varshney's *Ethnic Conflict and Civic Life*. The main focus of his study was why some cities were less prone to this form of violence than others. Though there are strong arguments against regarding India as a whole as a deeply divided society, his findings do have considerable relevance to deeply divided societies. Varshney found that, in accounting for the difference between communal peace and violence, 'the pre-existing local networks of civic engagement between the two communities stand out as the single most important *proximate* cause'. He went on:

> Where such networks of engagement exist, tensions and conflicts were regulated and managed; when they are missing, communal identities led to endemic and ghastly violence [. . .] [T]hese networks can be broken down into two parts: *associational* forms of engagement and *everyday* forms of engagement. The former ties are formed in organizational settings; the latter require no organization. Both forms of engagement, if intercommunal, promote peace, but the capacity of the associational forms to withstand nation-level "exogenous shocks" – such as India's partition in 1947 or the demolition of the Baburi mosque in December 1992 in full public gaze by Hindu militants – is substantially higher. (Varshney 2002: 9)

His conclusion can be seen as an argument in favour of integrationist policies to build such networks. It also highlights why deeply divided societies might be vulnerable to the deadly ethnic riot, since a common feature of these societies is the presence of very few, if any, organisations at a local level that cut across the society's fault line.

In contrast to Varshney's sociological perspective, Paul Brass puts forward a political analysis of what he calls the institutionalised riot system in India. Brass argues that the presentation of the riot as a spontaneous outburst between Hindu and Muslim crowds ignores the organisational role of militant Hindu groups in the violence.

> [I]n all cases of large-scale collective violence, we need to be attentive not only to the action taking place, but to the discourse about it. We need to note the phases and stages of production of collective violence and the deliberate testing of boundaries that take place in their production, the actions that confound our labels, the transgressions that signal the movement from one extreme form of violence to another, even more extreme form. We need finally to pay attention to the talk that takes place afterwards, including our own, that obfuscates rather than enlightens, that seeks precise definition and "causes" rather than exposure of what is concealed, that contributes to the violence by hiding more than it reveals. (Brass 2006: 8)

What is easily obscured in the characterisation of riots as between two groups is that most of the victims will commonly come from one community, and in all likelihood this will be from the weaker, minority community. The pattern is likely to be somewhat different in deeply divided societies, even where the division is horizontal rather than vertical. In deeply divided societies, both communities are likely to possess the capacity to inflict violence on the other. In the circumstances, riots are likely to be the prelude to other, more fully organised forms of violence. In this context, it is worth noting that the riots that marked the start of Northern Ireland's troubles in 1968 preceded the formation of the principal republican and loyalist paramilitary organisations, the Provisional Irish Republican Army and the Ulster Defence Association. Similarly, deadly ethnic riots preceded Sri Lanka's civil war.

Brass is also insistent on highlighting the role that inadequate and partisan law enforcement plays in the production and reproduction of riots, asserting:

> [T]hey could not have been carried out with such force in so many places, in many cases for extended periods of time, and repeatedly, without the complicity of the police and the failure of the political parties in control of government and the administrative and police officers in the district to prevent riots or at least contain them once they had begun. (Brass 2006: xv–xvi)

The next chapter follows on from this one by examining the immense challenge that the policing of deeply divided societies presents.

4 THE CHALLENGE OF POLICING

The subject of this chapter is the maintenance of order in a deeply divided society. In most societies, including deeply divided ones, primary responsibility for the maintenance of order is vested in the police. However, in part because the maintenance of order looms so large as a problem in deeply divided societies, this task may not be the exclusive concern of the police and the security forces may encompass a wider range of actors than simply ordinary members of the police, whether divided up on a regional basis or part of a single national institution. Deeply divided societies are not the only category of society in which the issue of policing is of central importance. That is also the case in post-conflict societies (which may of course also be deeply divided societies). Bruce Barker has described most eloquently why it matters so much:

> The establishment of security, order and adherence to the law is central to the building of post-conflict governance and a lasting peace. Without this framework new political and economic institutions will not take root. With no security, former combatants are not going to disarm; investors are not going to be attracted; new governments will not maintain their support; elections will not be free; crime waves will not be prevented; and mob justice and other forms of illegal non-state security will not be curbed (Barker 2004).

As the Americans and the British have discovered in Afghanistan and Iraq, overthrowing regimes is relatively easy. It requires only the possession of sufficient military strength to overwhelm a rogue regime, particularly if the invaders are assisted by local allies, as was the case in Afghanistan. However, constructing a viable political order is a task of an altogether different and more difficult kind. And it may prove virtually impossible in cases where there is widespread rejection of the legitimacy of the occupying powers.

Typology of Strategies for Maintaining Order

However, before consideration is given to the special challenges that deeply divided societies present for the maintenance of order, it is worth examining the different approaches that may be taken in any society to the maintenance of order. For this purpose a typology first developed for a multi-authored book on state strategies for maintaining order will be used (Brewer et al. 1988: 230–2). The typology was based on how a simple question was answered. Did the state treat politically motivated violent offenders more leniently or more harshly than offenders without such motivation or simply the same as such offenders? It is worth underlining that a characteristic of deeply divided societies is that a distinction tends to be made between prisoners on the basis of their motivation. Thus, in the case of Northern Ireland, prisoners without a political motivation for their actions are commonly referred to as ordinary decent criminals.

The approach of treating politically motivated violent offenders the same as ordinary decent criminals may be labelled criminalisation. It entails the use of the criminal law in relation to public disorder. It involves disregarding the political motivation behind a breach of the law and treating such an act the same way as any other breach of the law would be treated. The obvious justification for this approach is the upholding of the rule of law, particularly the requirement of equality before the law. From this perspective, the same rules should apply to all. In a situation in which the state is faced with a violent rebellion, it amounts to a policy of containment. In relation to ordinary crime, containment is an acceptable strategy, since no one expects the state to be able to prevent all crime. It is broadly accepted that the state cannot anticipate criminal behaviour in many instances and that the state's role conducted through the police is to ensure that criminals are brought to justice and punished for their actions. An advantage of applying the same approach to political violence is that it enables the state to claim, in its dealings with the outside world, that no fundamental political breakdown has occurred that would necessitate any departure from the rule of law. The assumption of normality also provides a basis on which the state can resist pressure to introduce measures to address the grievances behind political violence. It enables the state to claim that no political crisis exists. This is usually only possible if the level of political violence is relatively low.

The approach of treating politically motivated violent offenders more leniently than ordinary decent criminals, to use Northern Ireland parlance, may be labelled accommodation. Its justification is that legitimate political grievances lie behind the outbreak of political violence. And it represents a strategy of seeking to quell disorder by addressing its fundamental causes. This usually means accepting that politically motivated violent offenders should be treated differently from those who resort to violence on their own behalf, for reasons unconnected to the political conflict. Accommodation commonly includes measures designed to reduce antagonism towards the authorities and to meet some of the demands of the insurgents. It also typically includes early prisoner release schemes and amnesties, especially in the context of ceasefires and the initiation of negotiations to end armed conflict.

The approach of treating politically motivated violent offenders more harshly than ordinary decent criminals may be described as suppression. Suppression, like accommodation, takes cognisance of the political motivation of those who resort to violence for collective purposes. However, unlike accommodation, it does not seek to appease offenders in this category but to repress them. The presence of a political motivation is seen as an aggravating factor that increases the threat posed to society and consequently justifies their being treated more harshly than ordinary decent criminals. Further, this approach quite commonly involves not just the harsh treatment of those directly implicated in acts of violence but also the repression of expressions of support for the rebels. Thus possession of a poster extolling the cause of the rebels may itself be made a criminal offence.

The three approaches are not mutually exclusive. Firstly, the state may simultaneously pursue different approaches in relation to the different threats it faces. For example, through the course of the first decade of the twenty-first century, the British government pursued a policy of accommodation in the context of the Northern Ireland peace process; a policy of criminalisation in relation to the activities of groups such as the Animal Liberation Front; and a policy of suppression in relation to the threat posed by global jihadis linked to al Qaeda. The pursuit of such different approaches was the cause of some critical comment and a number of journalists questioned in particular the logic of the sharp distinction the government drew between the Provisional Irish Republican Army and al Qaeda. Secondly, at different times, the government may pursue all three of the different approaches in relation to the same problem, depending on the particular phase of the conflict. Thus, in the early stages of the Northern Ireland conflict, the government's approach was one of suppression. That was followed by one of criminalisation as the level of violence fell. Another factor that encouraged the adoption of this approach was the failure of the government's efforts to achieve a political settlement. Finally, with the dawn of the peace process and the possibility of bringing the conflict to an end, criminalisation gave way to accommodation as the government sought to provide incentives for those in paramilitary organisations to turn away from violence permanently.

Each of the approaches has its own limitations. Consequently, few governments pursue one or other of these approaches on an entirely consistent basis. State strategies for dealing with political violence tend to evolve through the course of a conflict. A common criticism of the criminalisation approach is that it ignores the political nature of the crisis engulfing a society afflicted by more than sporadic acts of political violence. By contrast, accommodation is frequently criticised as a strategy to appease those engaged in political violence. A common objection to suppression is that it fails to address the underlying causes of the violence in seeking simply to prevent violence through the use of repressive methods. There is substance to each of these points. Devising effective strategies to deal with political violence without detracting from the legitimacy of the state presents an immense challenge in any society. It is even more difficult to achieve in a deeply divided one.

In their book *The Politics of Ethnic Conflict Regulation*, John McGarry and Brendan O'Leary set out a taxonomy of ethnic conflict regulation methods that is broad enough to be applied to deeply divided societies in general (McGarry and O'Leary 1993: 4). They organise these methods under two headings: methods for eliminating differences and methods for managing differences – and they identify four principal methods under each heading. Under methods of eliminating differences, they include genocide; forced mass population transfers; partition and secession; integration and assimilation. Under methods of managing differences they list hegemonic control; arbitration and third-party intervention; cantonisation and federalisation; and consociationalism and power-sharing. Their taxonomy may usefully be combined with the typology of state strategies for maintaining order, though with the inclusion, as an additional category, of the context of state breakdown. The result of combining the two lists is set out in Table 4.1.

Of the different forms of ethnic conflict regulation identified by McGarry and O'Leary, that of genocide was discussed in Chapter 3. Integration and assimilation are the focus of the next chapter, while partition, secession

Table 4.1   Combining forms of ethnic conflict regulation with state strategies/outcomes

Criminalisation	Accommodation	Suppression	Breakdown
integration and/or assimilation	*consociationalism or power-sharing*	*hegemonic control*	*partition and/ or secession*
cantonisation and/ or federalisation	*arbitration (third-party intervention)*	*genocide*	*genocide*
	cantonisation and/ or federalisation	*forced mass population transfers*	*forced mass population transfers*

and forced mass population transfer are examined in Chapter 6. This chapter also considers less drastic territorial approaches to conflict – approaches such as federalism and autonomy. What McGarry and O'Leary include under methods of managing differences – namely power-sharing and third-party mediation – is explored in Chapters 7 and 8. In this chapter the focus is on the security dimensions of these different forms of conflict regulation. It is also an appropriate place to examine in greater depth hegemony, or what Lustick called control, since security looms especially large under this form of conflict regulation.

Though the most extreme forms of violence – such as genocide and ethnic cleansing or forced mass population transfer – tend to be associated with suppression or the anarchic conditions of state breakdown, the extent of visible coercion and the level of political violence do not provide reliable indicators of the strategy being pursued by a state. Thus, suppression is at its most effective when relatively little coercion is required to ensure the outward appearance of calm, simply because overt challenges to the authorities have been snuffed out and there is little expectation on the part of the opposition that the state can be safely or effectively challenged through any form of violence. Even in deeply divided societies, which are characterised by contestation over the legitimacy of political authority, dominant communities may be able to exercise control over the society for long periods of time and sustain what Frank Wright described as tranquillity rather than peace.

In fact, as a broad generalisation, the formation of new regimes and the demise of old ones tend to be associated both with surges in political violence and with high levels of overt coercion. Because it is difficult to calculate the consequences of actions taken in such periods, the temptation to take risks so as to seize the moment is considerable. Maintaining order in these circumstances inevitably places considerable strain on the state's security forces. That may be compounded by simultaneous changes in their mission as a result of political change. One result can be the politicisation of the security forces themselves, and in extreme cases military intervention in the form of a coup. Transitions are often dangerous times, a point that will be returned to further below.

In his comparative study of the reform of security in settler societies, Ronald Weitzer identifies a number of features of the security systems of settler societies. He regards what he dubs 'sectarian security systems' as characteristic not just of settler societies, but also of communally divided societies. In short, his account can be applied to deeply divided societies, at least those that are divided horizontally, between a dominant and a subordinate community. According to Weitzer,

> A sectarian security system displays the following features:
>
> * a concentration of power and resources within the security state sector, which contributes to its *autonomous* position over other state branches;
> * a tendency to pursue order and maintain relations of dominance in a highly *repressive* fashion, unleavened by considerations of justice, legitimacy and basic human rights;
> * a *partisan* orientation on behalf of the dominant sector of society, instead of the collective interests of the wider population of the nation-state. (Weitzer 1990: 4)

Weitzer argues that the first two features are commonly found in authoritarian systems in general, but that 'its communally partisan orientation is specific to the sectarian model' (ibid.). The task of reform, as Weitzer sees it, is the liberalisation of these features of the model through the establishment of mechanisms to ensure accountability, respect for the rule of law and commitment to the impartial enforcement of the law.

The Case of Northern Ireland

To explore these propositions further, the evolution of policing in three cases of deeply divided societies is examined below. There are counter-intuitive aspects to this evolution in each case, underlining that historical circumstance can affect the way in which any model operates in practice. One of the cases Weitzer used for his study – that of Northern Ireland – will be examined first. Northern Ireland – with its own parliament and government – came into existence under the 1920 Government of Ireland Act partitioning colonial Ireland. It was originally intended under the Act that the existing police force for the whole of the island would simply be divided to serve the two new political entities. However, nationalist rejection of the Act, particularly as it affected the Southern 26 counties, forced the British government to accept the more radical step of the disbandment of the Royal Irish Constabulary (RIC). One consequence was the creation of a new police force for Northern Ireland, the Royal Ulster Constabulary (RUC).

Admittedly the new force was designed to attract former members of the RIC, as this helped to reduce its costs. Partly as a consequence of this objective, it was even envisaged that up to a third of the force would be Catholic. In practice this was never achieved. At their peak as a proportion of the force, Catholics constituted just over 20 per cent of the RUC in 1923. This had fallen to a little over 10 per cent at the time of the onset of the troubles in 1968. Under Unionist Party rule there was a close relationship between the police and the government. Close ties also existed between the police and the Orange Order, the organisation that mobilised Protestants in defence of the Union and religious freedom against Irish nationalism and the Catholic church. This was reflected in the establishment of an Orange lodge specifically catering for police membership.

Two other aspects of policing caused controversy during the period of unionist rule: the inclusion within the police of the Ulster Special Constabulary, generally known after its main component as 'the B Specials'; and the draconian powers accorded to the police under legislation initially enacted as a temporary emergency measure. The B Specials was a wholly Protestant part-time force – established to deal with the emergency of 1920 – that was recruited largely though the wartime Ulster Volunteer Force (UVF). The Civil Authorities (Special Powers) Act came into force in 1922. The Special Powers Act, as it was called, required renewal on an annual basis. This was done until 1928, when the Act was extended for a further five years. In 1933 it was made permanent and remained in force until 1972, when it was repealed by the British government after the imposition of direct rule from London. The Act contained Orwellian provisions that listed offences against the maintenance of law and order and then provided that any other acts that undermined law and order, but were not listed, were also offences under the legislation.

Repeal of the Special Powers Act and disbandment of the B Specials were among the main demands of the civil rights movement that challenged the unionist ascendancy in Northern Ireland in the 1960s. Indeed the issue of security played a central role in the onset of 'the troubles' – the term used to describe Northern Ireland's protracted violent conflict between

the 1960s and the 1990s. There is some variation in what events to treat
as the starting point of the troubles, including sectarian killings in 1966 or
the formation of the Northern Ireland Civil Rights Association in 1967.
However, the troubles are most commonly dated from 5 October 1968, a
day of clashes between the police and civil rights demonstrators in Lon-
donderry/Derry (Bew and Gillespie 1999). Further disturbances followed
and in August 1969, after the local security forces had been overwhelmed
by the scale of the unrest, the Unionist Party government in Northern
Ireland was forced to turn to the British government for assistance. As a
consequence, British troops were dispatched to the province in aid of the
civil power.

Police statistics on deaths as a result of the troubles date from 1969.
Despite the paramilitary ceasefires in 1994 and the conclusion of the
Belfast Agreement, they continue to be collected. The annual figures for
1969 to 2010 are given in Table 4.2. They show a pattern that is commonly
found in many conflicts, of a very rapid escalation in the first years of the
conflict. After a peak is reached, violence continues at a lower but relatively constant level. In the early phase the emphasis of the authorities
tends to be on the suppression of the violence, just as those seeking to

Table 4.2   Deaths due to the Northern Ireland security situation

Year	Police	Reserve	Army	UDR/RIR	Civilians	Total
1969	1	0	0	0	13	14
1970	2	0	0	0	23	25
1971	11	0	43	5	115	174
1972	14	3	105	26	322	470
1973	10	3	58	8	173	252
1974	12	3	30	7	168	220
1975	7	4	14	6	216	247
1976	13	10	14	15	245	297
1977	8	6	15	14	69	112
1978	4	6	14	7	50	81
1979	9	5	38	10	51	113
1980	3	6	8	9	50	76
1981	13	8	10	13	57	101
1982	8	4	21	7	57	97
1983	9	9	5	10	44	77
1984	7	2	9	10	36	64
1985	14	9	2	4	26	55

Table 4.2   (Continued)

Year	Police	Reserve	Army	UDR/RIR	Civilians	Total
1986	10	2	4	8	37	61
1987	9	7	3	8	68	95
1988	4	2	21	12	55	94
1989	7	2	12	2	39	62
1990	7	5	7	8	49	76
1991	5	1	5	8	75	94
1992	2	1	4	2	76	85
1993	3	3	6	2	70	84
1994	3	0	1	2	56	62
1995	1	0	0	0	8	9
1996	0	0	1	0	14	15
1997	3	1	1	0	17	22
1998	1	0	1	0	53	55
1999	0	0	0	0	7	7
2000	0	0	0	0	18	18
2001	0	0	0	0	17	17
2002	0	0	0	0	13	13
2003	0	0	0	0	11	11
2004	0	0	0	0	5	5
2005	0	0	0	0	5	5
2006	0	0	0	0	3	3
2007	0	0	0	0	3	3
2008	0	0	0	0	1	1
2009	1	0	2	0	2	5
2010	0	0	0	0	2	2
TOTALS	**201**	**102**	**454**	**203**	**2,419**	**3,379**

Police	Royal Ulster Constabulary
Reserve	Royal Ulster Constabulary Reserve
UDR	Ulster Defence Regiment
RIR	Royal Irish Regiment
CIVILIANS	including members of illegal paramilitary organisations

Source http://www.psni.police.uk

bring about political change through violence concentrate their efforts on achieving a rapid breakthrough. If the conflict does not end at this stage, the likelihood is of a levelling off of the violence, with a change in emphasis – towards sustaining the campaign of violence on the one hand and adjusting to the existence of a protracted conflict on the other.

The price of London's support for the government of Northern Ireland in 1969 was that there should be reform. In October of that year, the British government published a report, the Hunt Committee report, which recommended far-reaching changes to civilianise policing in Northern Ireland. It reflected the view expressed in the national media that the partisanship of the RUC had been a significant factor in aggravating the crisis. Indeed, leaving the unionist government in place while pressing it to introduce reforms underlined that the government in London perceived the crisis primarily as due to the breakdown of the security system rather than of the whole political system. The effect was to radicalise Catholic opinion, which feared that, after reforms designed to model the RUC after their counterparts in other parts of the United Kingdom, the unionist hegemony would be left in place for decades to come. The security situation steadily worsened, matters coming to a head after the unionist government introduced internment without trial, which produced a sharp escalation in the level of political violence.

Following the events of Bloody Sunday at the end of January 1972, in which British paratroopers shot dead a number of civilians in a riot following a civil rights demonstration, the British government recognised the need for root and branch changes to the political system and to this end imposed direct rule in March 1972. Initially the British government relied on the army as the primary body to quell political violence. But, after the failure of a number of political initiatives seeking to replace unionist rule with a power-sharing government representative of both unionists and nationalists, there was a change of course by the British government. It banked on the desire of the public in Northern Ireland for a return to normality, and in this context detention without trial was ended and the RUC was given primary responsibility for maintaining law and order. Direct rule was presented as the least unacceptable basis for the governance of the province, instead of a stop-gap designed to allow space for negotiations among the local parties. The new approach amounted to a strategy of criminalisation.

But the government's hopes for a decline in support for the IRA and other paramilitary organisations were not realised, particularly as a result of the polarisation of opinion in the province over the demands of republican prisoners for a restoration of political status that had been ended under the strategy of criminalisation. The crisis in the prisons in the early

1980s prompted the British government to seek the support of the Irish government in the management of the conflict. This was institutionalised under an international agreement, the Anglo-Irish Agreement of November 1985. And it became the linchpin of the government's policy in Northern Ireland, notwithstanding unionist protests directed at forcing its abandonment. Anglo-Irish conflict management bore fruit in the 1990s with the paramilitary ceasefires of 1994, which were eventually followed by the Belfast Agreement of April 1998. This provided for the replacement of direct rule by a power-sharing government representative of the major political parties in the province. However, the implementation of the Belfast Agreement encountered a series of problems, and it was only in 2010 that the last of these was overcome.

Through all these phases of policy from the onset of the troubles in the late 1960s, reform of policing was a constant theme. In the early years of the troubles, the emphasis was on bringing the RUC into line with the modernisation of police forces that had taken place in the rest of the United Kingdom, as well as on overcoming the RUC's reputation as a partisan force. Under direct rule, two aspects of policing were seen as key to securing acceptance of the police as impartial upholders of the law: operational autonomy and professionalisation. The former was intended to reduce political pressure on the police from unionists; the latter, to convince the public that their community background would not affect how the police officers behaved.

This approach had limited success in securing nationalist support, especially with the militarisation of the police under the policy of police primacy. Further, despite the government's efforts to foster a professional police force free of sectarian bias, Catholics who joined the RUC found evidence, in some parts of the force, not merely of religious prejudice but of sympathy for loyalist paramilitary organisations (Sheehy 2008: 44). Under the Anglo-Irish Agreement the Irish government was able to raise nationalist concerns on policing, and that put pressure on the RUC to take more account of nationalist opinion. More fundamental change came during the peace process, and especially as a result of the report of the Patten Commission (Independent Commission on Policing in Northern Ireland 1999).

The Patten Commission was set up under the terms of the Belfast Agreement, which provided that a commission on policing with international input be established to recommend changes to policing in the light of the political settlement. Its report was published in September 1999. Its recommendations included a change in the name of the police, and in due course the name of the force was changed from RUC to 'Police Service of Northern Ireland' (PSNI). Another key recommendation was that active steps should be taken through the recruitment process to increase Catholic representation in the force, so that the police would become more representative of the province's divided society. In particular, the Patten Commission proposed that Catholics should form 50 per cent of all new recruits.

The report angered unionists, and attempts by the British government to address some of their concerns led to republican complaints that the implementation of the report was being diluted by the government. But in fact the government did not back down on the implementation of the most important aspects of the Patten Report, including its radical proposal for increasing the number of Catholics in the police. From under 10 per cent of the force in 2001, the proportion of Catholics in the PSNI rose to nearly 30 per cent in 2010 (Moriarty 2010). Policing was a major issue in the renegotiation of the Belfast Agreement that led to the St Andrews Agreement in 2006. The prospect of the re-establishment of the power-sharing government persuaded Sinn Féin to endorse the PSNI in January 2007. However, the failure of the Democratic Unionist Party (DUP), by this point the majority party among unionists, to agree to the early devolution of policing and justice powers, as envisaged under the St Andrews Agreement, led to a fresh crisis in the peace process. The issue was finally resolved under the Hillsborough Agreement of February 2010, under which the devolution of policing and justice powers took place in April 2010.

The Case of Israel/Palestine

It is instructive to compare what has happened in Northern Ireland with the history of policing in Israel/Palestine, especially considering the parallels between the two cases as deeply divided societies. These include the origin of the political entities in partition; the siege mentality of the dominant community in the two societies; and the similarity of their conflicts as a clash between two nationalisms. The commonalities between the two cases has not gone unnoticed, at least in Northern Ireland, and this is reflected in unionist identification with the Israeli cause and Irish nationalist identification with that of the Palestinians. Thus, when the prime minister of Israel, Ariel Sharon, launched a military assault on the Palestinian Authority in March 2002, thousands upon thousands of Israeli flags were flown from lamp-posts in hardline unionist neighbourhoods across Northern Ireland. It was a way for many unionists to express their preference for the approach taken by Sharon towards the Palestinians over what they saw as the British government's appeasement of Irish Republicans.

The Israel Police came into existence at the inception of the state of Israel. It came under the authority of a separate ministry of police. However, this was not a sign of the high status or importance attached to the police, but just the opposite. The portfolio had a low standing within the government. It was created because the minister of the interior did not want responsibility for the police, which he regarded as a liability. What explained his attitude was that the Israel Police had the misfortune to be seen as the successor of the Palestinian Police, the police force created by the British during their rule of the territory under a League of Nations Mandate. This force was poorly regarded by members of the Jewish community. In addition, the attitudes that Jewish immigrants brought with them towards the police as an institution tended to be based on the experience of their treatment as a minority that was commonly discriminated against if not subject to even worse treatment. A consequence of these attitudes was that limited responsibilities were initially vested in the Israel Police. In particular, the Israel Defence Forces (IDF) were accorded primary responsibility for security. This was supplemented by intelligence gathering of the General Security Service commonly referred to as Shin Bet, which was responsible to the office of the prime minister and not to the ministry of police, and by the separate Border Police, established in 1953 to guard the country's frontiers.

Between 1948 and 1966 Palestinians in Israel were subject to military rule under emergency regulations inherited from the last years of the British mandate. After 1966 the emergency regulations were invoked from time to time to deal with specific situations. For example, military rule was re-imposed in some areas during the Six-Day War in 1967 and the regulations were employed to place a number of Palestinian villages under curfew during the 1976 Land Day protests. The territories Israel occupied as a result of the 1967 war were subject to military rule until Israel's partial withdrawal from the territories under the Oslo peace process in the 1990s. However, until the first Palestinian intifada in 1987, a minor role in the policing of the West Bank was played by members of the Jordanian police under co-option by the Israeli authorities. From the perspective of the Israeli government, this was an ideal arrangement for reducing the burden of occupation, since it did not place Israel's overall strategic control of the territories in any jeopardy. It came to an end as a result of mass resignations from the force during the first intifada.

In 1974 the Israel Police was given responsibility for internal security, but even its Special Duties Division, the police's principal agency in the fight against terrorism, has tended to take second place to Shin Bet. And, despite the extension to the police's remit, its primary responsibility has been seen as one of fighting crime. In fact, concern over soaring crime rates in the 1970s provided the main impetus for change in the force. It led to the appointment of a commission on the issue and, when its recommendations failed to quell concern over crime rates, to the adoption of the Tirosh Plan to expand the size of police force. But the relatively low priority of policing despite this impetus was reflected in the fact that expenditure by the ministry of police remained at less than 1 per cent of total government expenditure.

The contrast in the role of the police in Israel/Palestine and Northern Ireland is very striking. Admittedly, the picture has become more complex as a result of the failed, or at least incomplete, peace process in Israel/Palestine that has spawned a number of different police forces across the whole of Israel/Palestine. The position within the occupied territories, the putative basis of a future Palestinian state, is especially complex, particularly in the light of the creeping annexation of part of the West Bank by settlements supported by Israel. It might be argued that Israel/Palestine is better described as a deeply divided territory than as a deeply divided society. The creation of two states would justify the implication that two separate societies had come into existence, but in advance of such a development the interdependence of the communities that currently inhabit Israel/Palestine is sufficient reason to retain the description of a deeply divided society for the whole area. That is not to suggest that the relationship between the Jewish and Palestinian is a symmetrical one. Indeed the relative impotence of the Palestinians remains, politically, a reason for questioning whether Israel will agree in the near future to the creation of a viable Palestinian state.

If the comparison of policing in Israel/Palestine and Northern Ireland is confined to comparing the Israel Police and the RUC/PSNI, the differences are stark. The Israel Police is not highly regarded. Pay in the police is low. The force has played a limited role in the maintenance of public order. While behaviour of the police has from time to time been the subject of criticism, it has not generally been at the centre of political debate about the future of Israel/Palestine. Issues such as the composition of the force and its role in a deeply divided society have largely escaped scrutiny. By contrast, police officers in Northern Ireland have been well remunerated. Members of the police have a high status in society, and through much of the troubles the RUC played the leading role in the maintenance of public order. At the same time the RUC was at the centre of political controversy, with republicans demanding its disbandment. The peace process has enabled a measure of civilianisation of policing to take place, though the activities of violent dissident groups have placed some strain on this transformation.

The explanation of the differences in the roles of the police force in the two cases is relatively straightforward. It suited Israel to present the threat to its security primarily in external terms, justifying the role of its army and thereby also portraying the conflict as a David and Goliath struggle between Israel and the Arab world rather than as a conflict within a deeply divided society, between Jews and Palestinians. Consequently check points, surveillance and the detention of suspects in the West Bank were – and continue to be – conducted by the Israeli Defence Forces. By contrast, the British government wished the outside world to view the conflict in Northern Ireland as an internal one, between Protestants and Catholics, since that perspective gave most legitimacy to the objective of British policy to secure political accommodation between the two communities within the context of Northern Ireland's existing boundaries.

The Case of South Africa

The third case to be examined, that of South Africa, has features in common with both Israel/Palestine and Northern Ireland, but it has followed a distinctly different trajectory in the course of the country's transformation into a non-racial democracy. Like the Royal Ulster Constabulary, the South African Police owed much to the British colonial model of policing. The South African Police (SAP) was established as a national force at the foundation of the Union of South Africa in 1910. It brought together the forces that had operated in the four colonies prior to union. In common with these, the SAP was a militarised force that had as its primary task the consolidation of white control of the country. From the very beginning, pay and conditions in the SAP were poor; however, the impoverishment of rural Afrikaners provided a constant stream of recruits. From the very beginning, the force also included Africans in its lower ranks. Successive governments exercised strong political control over the actions of the force, and that was reflected in its use against strikes of white workers, most notably in 1922. The police was also used to enforce the laws that were introduced to control the influx of Africans into the urban areas, a process that the authorities viewed as a threat to white political domination.

A commission of inquiry into policing problems in the 1930s graphically described the resulting attitudes towards the police in the country's townships.

We are of the opinion, after a careful survey of the evidence, that the relations between natives and police are marked by a suppressed hostility which

> excludes whole-hearted co-operation [. . .] This is due partly to the odium
> incurred by the police in enforcing unpopular legislation, but is contributed
> to by the manner in which such enforcement is carried out and the general
> attitude of some individual policemen to the native population. (Quoted in
> Cawthra 1993: 11)

In short, the reputation of the police for brutality and racism long preceded
the election victory of the National Party on a platform of apartheid
in 1948.

Under apartheid, policing became even more authoritarian and suppres-
sive. The tightening of the National Party government's grip on power led
to the Afrikanerisation of the senior ranks of the police and to a vast extension of the powers of the police. It also led to expansion in the size of the
force and to the increasing recruitment of blacks into the lower ranks of
the police. However, the focus of the police on maintaining white domination – serving the interests of whites more generally and enforcing controls
over the movement of the African population and other apartheid regulations rather than combating ordinary crime – remained unchanged. Their
role under apartheid is well summarised by Mark Shaw.

> Little attempt was made by the police to reduce crime in black areas, the
> majority of police resources being concentrated in white towns and suburbs.
> Black people were policed for control and not crime prevention; the police
> aimed to prevent crime in white areas not by reducing it in black areas but
> by preventing the uncontrolled movement of black people, who were con-
> sidered to be its perpetrators. Thus, the police spent an inordinate amount
> of resources on arresting people for apartheid administrative offences, such
> as not being in possession of a 'pass' in a white area, but seldom confronted
> criminal violence in the townships themselves. (Shaw 2002: 1)

South Africa under apartheid fitted perfectly the model, set out in Chapter
3, of indifference from the authorities, in a horizontally divided society,
towards crime where both perpetrator and victim come from the subordinate community.

While, as in Israel, the status of the police was low and the pay and
conditions of its members were relatively poor, the police did have the
major role in security, in contrast to the situation in Israel. The four and a
half decades of National Party rule were marked by an intensification of
suppression up to 1990, the year in which the transition to a new dispensation began. The 1950 Suppression of Communism Act was used to target
a wide range of the government's opponents, while providing the basis
for the actions of an increasingly powerful security police. After the

Sharpeville massacre in 1960, the African National Congress (ANC) and the Pan-Africanist Congress (PAC) were outlawed. Detention without trial for up to 90 days in solitary confinement was introduced in 1963. In its wake there was a spate of allegations of torture by the Security Police. The police was also at the forefront of suppressing the Soweto uprising of 1976, which evolved out of protests by secondary school children. Under P. W. Botha's total strategy in the 1980s a larger role was given to the military in confronting the revolt in the African townships that followed the establishment of the tricameral parliament, but the army supplemented rather than replaced the actions of the police. And through the 1980s the police played the leading role in the organisation of hit squads for the assassination of anti-apartheid activists.

The transition from apartheid to a new political dispensation represented a huge challenge for the SAP, and this was clearly recognised by President de Klerk when he embarked on the transition in 1990. He addressed senior police officers in January 1990 in advance of his announcement of the release of Nelson Mandela from jail and the removal of the bans on the ANC, PAC and South African Communist Party. He explained that henceforth their role would be to combat ordinary crime in accordance with the role of police forces all over the world, but that in future they would no longer be asked to perform a political control function, as they had in the past. The government had good reason for concern over how the police might react to the steps it was taking to create the context for negotiations with the ANC, since the police was widely seen as a bastion of support for the government's extreme right opponents in the Conservative Party and in the Afrikaner Weerstandsbeweging (AWB – Afrikaner Resistance Movement).

The four years of South Africa's transition, from Mandela's release from prison to his inauguration as president, were the most violent in the country's history. This is underscored by the monthly totals of those killed in political violence that were compiled by the South African Institute of Race Relations and are shown in Table 4.3. Elements within the security forces from both the military and the police continued to be involved in the violent power struggle taking place inside the country alongside the constitutional negotiations among the political parties. The extent to which they acted at the behest of, or under the control of, the National Party government remains a matter of debate. The term 'the third force' was widely used to describe such elements. It encapsulated a measure of uncertainty over where ultimate responsibility for their actions lay. However, towards the end of the transition, senior police officers accused of involvement in stoking violence in the townships as a result of inquiries into the ongoing violence were purged from the force. Further, through the

Table 4.3   Monthly totals of political fatalities in South Africa, 1985 to 1996*

	Jan	Feb	Mar	Apr	May	Jun	Jul	Aug	Sep	Oct	Nov	Dec	Total
1985	4	35	76	46	66	45	96	163	69	86	101	92	879
1986	105	112	179	145	221	212	122	76	40	16	37	33	1298
1987	40	22	40	40	33	36	39	35	73	93	89	121	661
1988	211	107	62	48	58	76	94	112	108	90	85	98	1149
1989	126	95	89	99	89	38	96	104	135	116	129	287	1403
1990	210	283	458	283	208	150	247	698	417	162	316	267	3699
1991	187	129	351	270	318	150	164	184	282	218	283	170	2706
1992	139	238	348	300	230	324	278	361	339	332	299	159	3347
1993	135	129	143	212	339	309	547	451	425	398	370	317	3749
1994	239	259	537	436	207	119	136	106	109	106	94	128	2476
1995	131	87	79	138	100	82	92	61	69	49	54	102	1044
1996	39	47	59	67	45	53	64	63	81	57	47	61	683

Total number of fatalities in 12 years of political violence: 23,094
* In the months September to November 1984 there were 149 fatalities.
SOURCE Elizabeth Sidiropoulos (ed.), *South Africa Survey 1996/97*, Johannesburg: South African Institute of Race Relations, 1997, p. 600

course of the transition, some steps were taken to instil into members of the police a sense of accountability for their actions. For example, under the National Peace Accord of 1991 police officers were required to wear name tags, while it was stipulated that police vehicle numbers should be clearly displayed.

The ANC's concerns about how the police might act when the party became the leading force in the Government of National Unity following the country's first democratic elections were eased by the fact that by this time blacks constituted a majority among members of the police. Further, the increasing detachment of black policemen from the old order was evident in their actions during the transition, including their participation in the Police and Prisons Civil Rights Union (POPCRU), which campaigned on issues of service delivery and racism as well as on working conditions. In the course of the multi-party negotiations on a new constitution, it was agreed that there would be a national police force covering the whole country. This meant the incorporation of the police forces that had been set up in the Bantustans. Also agreed was a small change in the name of the force, so the SAP became the South African Police Service (SAPS). Various other cosmetic changes were introduced, in an effort to create a new image for the police.

The ANC never regarded the police in post-apartheid South Africa as a threat to its rule. Consequently, the question of policing did not receive the same level of attention as was accorded, for example, to the future of the military. The hope and expectation was that the police would quickly secure the trust of the public as its focus shifted to the legitimate task of fighting crime. It was recognised that the police's brutal methods in the past had damaged its standing, but it was assumed that its conduct in the future would be guided by the human rights norms of the new democracy. However, the leaders of the ANC grossly underestimated the obstacles to such a transformation. In particular, they failed to appreciate that the poorly trained and equipped force that the country had inherited from white minority rule lacked the capacity to fulfil the role they envisaged. At the same time, the spread of crime from the townships to the suburbs drew attention to the country's very high levels of crime, and their continuance appeared as a major failing of the new dispensation, though the vast majority of victims of crime were poor and black, as they had been in the past.

A 2008 account of policing in post-apartheid society – which is based on observations, on the ground, of police operations – underscores the fundamental problems South Africa still faced on policing, more than a decade after the establishment of the country's non-racial democracy. Jonny Steinberg's study is remarkably stark in its judgements of why policing is not working. His point of departure, highly pertinent to all deeply divided societies, is that the 'most important precondition for policing in a democratic society is the consent of the general population to be policed' (Steinberg 2008: 20). Further, he argues when such consent is not forthcoming,

> in one way or another, the police retreat. They either avoid policing in those zones where they are not welcome . . . Or they use one or another means to negotiate their presence in those zones. To negotiate usually means to sell something: information, the obstruction of justice, the assurance they will not intervene. (Steinberg 2008: 21)

Steinberg accepts that there are many reasons why the police in post-apartheid South Africa has failed to secure the moral authority needed for policing by consent. He notes that township residents he interviewed for his study emphasised two in particular.

> The first is that the police were never forgiven for their role under apartheid. They returned to the townships in the early 1990s a disgraced and ingratiating bunch, and never recovered their dignity, certainly never enough to become the agents by whom the general population would consent to being policed.
>   Second, police officers find themselves somewhere near the tail end of a frantic, unseemly dash to join the new black middle class [. . .] The police are among a large category of township people who aspire very much to find a place in this class, who do not earn quite enough to get there, and who thus live beyond their means. They are, as a consequence, widely reputed in township life to be among a new breed of scavengers, prone to corruption and to the most expedient and instrumental attitudes to their own vocation. (Steinberg 2008: 23–4)

However, it is worth underlining that the obstacles Steinberg identifies to policing by consent in post-apartheid South Africa are by no means of the kind that are only to be found in deeply divided societies. They do reflect the problems that societies in political transition more generally encounter.

Vertically Divided Societies

Hitherto the focus of this chapter has been on cases of horizontally divided societies. The cases examined were most similar during the phase when a dominant community sought to maintain a position of hegemony over the society and the subordinate community was denied any share of political power. Only Israel within the green line (in other words, excluding the West Bank and Gaza) still fits that description. Since the era of dominant community control ended in South Africa and Northern Ireland, policing has followed somewhat different trajectories in the three cases examined in this chapter. The pattern in vertically divided societies is even more varied than in horizontally divided ones. The composition, function and status of the police owe much to the history of the society in question. Under colonial rule it was common for the police to be recruited from minority communities or from those on the periphery of the society, on the grounds that their dependence on the authorities would ensure their loyalty. For example, in Cyprus the British colonial authorities recruited the police from the Turkish Cypriot minority on the island. A consequence was that the struggle of the Greek Cypriot majority against colonial rule in the 1950s inevitably exacerbated divisions between the island's two communities.

A strategy states may employ when seeking to rule large territories containing a number of dispersed communities of one kind or another is to devolve policing to the regions. Where a police force is recruited locally in a particular area and is made accountable to the regional rather than the national government, that may assist the process of securing policing by consent. An example is the Ertzaintza in the Basque autonomous region in Spain. It was established as part of devolution of power from the centre following the end of the Franco dictatorship. Though derided by radical Basque nationalists and not entirely trusted by Spanish national governments, the force was far more acceptable to most people in the Basque region than national police units such as the Civil Guard were. Another, more contentious example was the creation of a Kosovan police force under the autonomy granted to the region under Tito's communist government. Complaints by the Serb minority in Kosovo about the conduct of this force played a significant role in Milošević's rise to power in Yugoslavia at the end of the Cold War.

The legitimacy and effectiveness of policing is an important issue in all societies. Professionalisation, the observance of human rights and the composition of the force have been seen as important in achieving the objective of policing by consent, though the relative importance attached to each has varied considerably according to circumstances and to prevailing opinion in the particular society. The issue of the composition of the police has tended to loom large in deeply divided societies, in which it is commonly held that the members of the police need to be broadly representative, in ethnic and racial terms, of the society they are policing. But that notion has also grown in influence as an aspect of multiculturalism, even in societies in which ethnic and racial minorities are not powerful enough to form the basis of the main cleavage in society. However, such societies rarely face as much difficulty in securing general public consent for policing as do deeply divided societies.

Symptomatic of that is the state's failure in deeply divided societies to establish a monopoly of legitimate violence. That makes it possible for organisations outside the control of the state to operate their own unofficial policing to rival that provided by the state. Examples can be found in all three of the cases discussed above. What is also characteristic of deeply divided societies is that the issue of securing consent for policing is not separable from the wider political context. In other words, as the cases of both South Africa and Northern Ireland demonstrate, limited headway in this direction is likely to be made in the absence of a comprehensive political settlement. But, as the South African case underlines, a political settlement may not be sufficient in itself to establish the basis for legitimate and effective policing under the authority of the state. Yet the problems to be found in South Africa are not unknown in other states in the Third World. And that begs another question. How really different are deeply divided societies? This issue is addressed in the next chapter.

5 LIMITS TO INTEGRATION

It might seem axiomatic that a key long-term objective of government policy in any deeply divided society should be the erosion of communal differences, so as to remove the very basis for division in the society and thus the central cause of conflict. However, attitudes towards the creation of homogeneous societies, particularly through imposition by government, have changed significantly, with an obvious bearing on this possibility. This not only applies to clearly reprehensible policies of expulsion, exclusion or ethnic cleansing, but it also extends to much more benign forms of social engineering. In particular, the notion that any government should seek to erase cultural differences among the population under its rule tends to be associated these days with unacceptable practices and doctrines of Western superiority. Thus in February 2008, in a statement in parliament, the Australian Prime Minister Kevin Rudd issued an apology to the country's indigenous population. He declared:

Today we honour the Indigenous peoples of this land, the oldest continuing cultures in human history. We reflect on their past mistreatment. We reflect in particular on the mistreatment of those who were stolen generations – this blemished chapter in our nation's history. The time has now come for the nation to turn a new page in Australia's history by righting the wrongs of the past and so moving forward with confidence to the future. We apologise for the laws and policies of successive Parliaments and governments that have inflicted profound grief, suffering and loss on these our fellow Australians. We apologise especially for the removal of Aboriginal and Torres Strait Islander children from their families, their communities and their country. For the pain, suffering and hurt of these stolen generations, their descendants and for their families left behind, we say sorry. To the mothers and the fathers, the brothers and the sisters, for the breaking up of families and communities, we say sorry. And for the indignity and degradation thus inflicted on a proud people and a proud culture, we say sorry. (Rudd 2008)

Rudd's statement exemplified two features of contemporary politics: firstly, the fashion for making apologies for past wrongs; and, secondly, the disrepute attached to policies of assimilation. Rudd's predecessor, John Howard, had expressed regret over what had been done to the aborigines but refused to go as far as to issue an apology. Howard had argued that an apology would run the danger of reinforcing an unhealthy culture of victimisation among the aborigines. But there was no dispute between the two leaders that the practices of the past had been wrong.

However, though few political leaders anywhere in the world these days openly defend policies of forced assimilation, pressure to make minorities conform to the norms of the majority has by no means disappeared. In fact, Australia provides a notable example of such pressure being applied. In 2007, in response to a report detailing widespread child abuse among aboriginal communities in the country's Northern Territory, Howard proclaimed that the situation was a national emergency and introduced a series of measures, including a ban on the sale of alcohol and the distribution of pornography in the communities in which rampant child abuse was taking place. Many other examples might be given of such pressures on matters small and large, from the headscarf ban in French schools to curbs on arranged marriages in Britain. Indeed, whenever the cultural practices of a minority, particularly an immigrant minority, clash with the norms of the majority or the mainstream and conflict results, there is likely to be pressure on members of the minority community to change their behaviour. But this needs to be seen in the context of a major change in attitudes towards the issue of cultural differences, which has been encapsulated in the concept of multiculturalism. While the interpretation of multiculturalism varies considerably from country to country, its adoption as a central aspect of many countries' policies towards minorities has meant that the principle has come to be widely recognised as a norm to which countries should adhere in their dealings with minorities.

Assimilation and Integration

To discuss these issues in greater depth, a brief consideration of some of the key terms used is necessary, including the notions of assimilation, acculturation, integration and multiculturalism. Assimilation is generally used to describe the process of absorption or incorporation of a group into a larger society through the group's acceptance of the norms and cultural practices of that larger society. In his 1992 typology of ethnic management strategies John Coakley described assimilation as 'the best-known and most widely practised of all ethnic management strategies' and gave the following account of the operation of the strategy in practice:

> In many parts of Europe there has been a powerful momentum towards the forcible assimilation of ethnic and linguistic minorities, typically by denying them access to political and cultural self-expression and by limiting the availability of educational facilities. Historical examples abound. Thus the British state sought to extend English cultural influence over its Celtic peripheries. Russia subjected its non-Russian peripheries to intense Russification pressures during the last decades of the old regime; and the spread of standard Italian throughout the Italian peninsula proceeded further after the completion of the unification process in 1870. Much more recently, strongly assimilative policies have been followed in very different contexts in France, Bulgaria and Romania. (Coakley 1992: 349)

He noted in addition that successful nationalist movements that had been subjected to assimilationist pressures were no less assiduous in the pursuit of homogeneity over their own realms. Coakley's typology consisted of a series of pairs, based on whether change originated with the state or from below. He then posed a number of questions, one of which was whether the culture of the group survived. He termed the two possibilities that arose if it did survive 'indigenization' and 'accommodation', while he attached the terms 'assimilation' and 'acculturation' to the two possibilities if it did not. However, it is worth noting that in practice assimilation and acculturation may be both gradual and partial processes, so some members of a group may be more susceptible to the pressure and/or appeal to throw in their lot with the wider society than the group is as a whole.

Coakley used 'indigenization' to refer to 'unsolicited state policies of cultivation of ethnic minorities in general' (1992: 346), while he employed the term 'accommodation' for situations in which the state sought to satisfy demands from below for the recognition of ethnic or other identities. Following the logic of his typology, he applied the term 'assimilation' to cases where the pressure came from the state, and 'acculturation' to cases where the desire for absorption originated from within the group itself. He gave as examples of acculturation the declining numbers of Gaelic speakers in Scotland and of Welsh speakers in Wales, 'despite a new benevolence on the part of the state' (p. 349). But, more pertinently from the perspective of this book, he suggested that the term might also be applied to the quest for equality of subordinate groups, with examples such as the American civil rights movement in the 1960s and the struggle of African nationalists for a non-racial society in South Africa.

It is worth underlining the point that the advantages of being accepted as full members of the majority community or of the mainstream of society provide a powerful incentive for acculturation on the part of members of any minority. This applies most obviously to immigrants who are commonly keen on being absorbed into the society in which they have settled as a means of upward mobility. Indeed, resistance to this process is more likely to come from members of the host society than from within the minority. In this context, acculturation may increase hostility towards immigrants among some sections of the host society, insofar as it equips such immigrants to compete more effectively in the labour market with members of the indigenous population. This will be the case particularly if the employment of immigrants in low-paid jobs appears to enable employers to reduce wage levels. However, the impact of this factor will be reduced if immigrants are absorbed into trade unions that ensure that employers are unable to exploit newcomers in this way. The particular circumstances of immigration matter and, consequently, the pattern of immigrant adaption to their host societies varies. But, commonly, the first generation of immigrants to a society is likely to want to secure its place in that society and is likely to find acculturation an attractive strategy in the pursuit of this objective.

The term 'integration' is most commonly used to describe the removal of barriers erected by government or society to the full acceptance of members of a minority, whether indigenous or immigrant, as equal citizens of the society. This explains why, despite the similarity of its meaning to assimilation, integration tends to have positive connotations. Thus integration is seen as the opposite of segregation, or, to put the point another way, as a synonym for desegregation. Though sometimes used in other contexts, such as the separation of men and women, segregation is most closely associated with discrimination against people on the grounds of race and colour, practices now generally condemned.

A further factor underpinning the legitimacy of integration as opposed to assimilation has been the assumption that the goal of integration is to achieve the participation of those being absorbed into the wider society on terms of equality. And, whereas it is assumed that assimilation of, say, members of group B into society A simply enlarges A through the conversion of Bs into As, integration between A and B produces a new entity, A + B. In practice, the contribution of group B may be a relatively small one, but there is clearly a difference in principle between the two outcomes. Esman sees this as the nub of the difference between assimilation and integration:

A fine line separates policies of assimilation [. . .] and integration. In both cases the intended outcome is a common culture and national society. Assimilation, however, implies that newcomers as well as indigenous minorities are to be absorbed by the host society without leaving any mark on that society. Integration, by contrast, is closer to the melting pot metaphor, implying that each wave of new arrivals makes its unique contribution to the ever-evolving whole. Elements of ethnic cultures survive, but these are shared by others, while all participate in an increasingly common culture and mixed society. (Esman 2004: 156)

Esman also makes a useful distinction between two dimensions of integration, the cultural and the social.

Cultural integration involves the adoption, for purposes of everyday communication, of the mainstream language, and of mainstream dress, cuisine, popular entertainment, and lifestyles. Social integration entails living in mixed neighbourhoods, participating in mainstream institutions such as churches and social clubs, and eventual inter-marriage. Cultural integration normally precedes the social by as much as several generations and individuals may spend their lifetimes culturally but not socially integrated. (Esman 2004: 159)

This might seem to be a slightly surprising conclusion, since the obstacles to cultural integration appear in many instances just as profound as those to social integration. The explanation for Esman's conclusion is to be found in part in the importance he attaches to the role of race. Thus he identifies the survival of racism, particularly in North America and Europe, as a significant obstacle to social integration. He refers to this 'informal racism' as a way of acknowledging that, for the most part, official sanction is not given to these attitudes and the discriminatory behaviour they give rise to. Racism of any kind tends to be repudiated in official discourse, particularly in countries where discrimination on the grounds of race was enshrined in government policy in one way or another prior to the 1960s. However, coded appeals to racism can be found in the stances taken by political parties in a number of countries in relation to issues such as immigration and the problematic question of how far society should seek to compensate members of minority communities for past discrimination through such measures as affirmative action.

Esman also notes that immigrants themselves may resist integration, particularly when they perceive the price of integration to be the abandonment of religious practices and customs in relation to dress and other matters that they regard as outward affirmations of their religious faith. Thus he notes the resistance of many Muslims from North Africa who live in France to becoming Frenchmen and women in the manner prescribed by the French authorities. But it might be objected that what is being resisted by Muslims in France, as well as in many other European countries, is not integration but assimilation. In societies such as the United States, in which there is a greater readiness to accommodate diversity within the bounds of a civic nationalism, there is considerable variation in the extent of both cultural and social integration. This is well described by Esman.

> Where ethnic communities are coterminous with a distinctive religious inheritance, as among Greeks, Armenians, Jews, and Sikhs, communal solidarity is strengthened and the process of integration is retarded, but not blocked. [. . .] The fact that the majority of young Jews in the United States now marry outside the faith demonstrates the powerful incentives and attractiveness of integrative behavior in that environment. The higher the levels of education and of social and occupational mobility, the more individuals are prone to leave their ethnic community behind. The remnants of several groups manage to survive as viable entities – for example, the Amish, the Hasidic Jews, Najavos, and other Indian nations – successfully resisting the appeal of the mainstream. Continuing immigration replenishes the ranks of Puerto Rican, Mexican, and Dominican communities, even as large numbers of their second and third generation intermarry and pass into mainstream. The principal exception is African–Americans, whose social integration in large numbers is blocked by persistent prejudice. (Esman 2004: 160)

Multiculturalism

A major landmark in the creation of an international consensus that racial discrimination was unacceptable was the American civil rights movement in the 1960s. It is perhaps not entirely coincidental that the concept of multiculturalism only took root after this consensus had been achieved, since in the absence of such a consensus multiculturalism might have been interpreted as a way of justifying racial discrimination on a new basis. Instead, multiculturalism has been seen as the means to prevent assimilation under the guise of integration. The idea of multiculturalism initially came to the fore in Canada in the early 1970s. It arose out of criticism of the earlier promotion of biculturalism as excluding Canada's first peoples, as well as many immigrants, from the ambit of a policy intended to underscore equality between anglophones and francophones. The essence of the policy was that the cultural diversity of the country's population should be seen as part of Canada's heritage and preserved within the broad framework of the commitment to bilingualism. It implied a picture of society as a mosaic of different cultures, with contact and exchange between the groups but the preservation of different ethnic identities. From Canada, multiculturalism spread as an approach to Australia, the United Kingdom, the Netherlands, and then to other countries in Europe and has been adopted in a number of countries as a basis for policy in the broad areas of race relations and the treatment of ethnic minorities. While not formally adopted as policy by the federal government in the United States, the idea of multiculturalism was influential there too in underpinning emphasis on cultural pluralism as one of America's strengths.

The idea had special appeal in countries in which racial discrimination had previously been officially tolerated. For example, until 1973, immigration to Australia had been explicitly restricted on the basis of race. The official adoption of multiculturalism helped to relegate the white Australia policy firmly to the past by providing a very different vision of the country's future development that no longer presented the country as a fragment of Europe in the Pacific. But, in spite of the concept's utility for a post-colonial era, multiculturalism has been widely criticised, particularly on the right and extreme right of the political spectrum. However, a distinction needs to be made in this context between simply the fact of the diversity of a country's population and response to this fact in terms of policy. For those on the extreme right, what is objectionable is the presence of racial and ethnic minorities in the society. Typically their focus is on factors that they blame for bringing about the diversity of the country's population. So commonly their objection to multiculturalism is coupled with demands to stop, and even to reverse immigration that adds to the size of the minorities.

Criticism of multiculturalism as a policy takes two main forms. Nationalists or those concerned with the country's political cohesion make the case that multiculturalism tends to encourage dual loyalties, particularly among immigrant minorities with ties to their countries of origin. In the case of Canada, this took the form of an objection to lending legitimacy to the notion of hyphenated Canadians. In the 1980s the Conservative Party government in the United Kingdom constantly criticised what it saw as the Labour Party's preoccupation with the promotion of ethnic minorities at the expense of the wishes of members of these minorities to be accepted as British. Multiculturalism as a policy has also been criticised from a liberal, integrationist perspective. These critics argue that, insofar as multiculturalism is associated with the static co-existence of different communities, it tends to detract from the objective of a common society in which there are equal opportunities for all. Further, it is argued that, in the case of groups disadvantaged by racial discrimination, multiculturalism may at best be irrelevant to their position in society and might at worst provide a rationale for informal segregation.

However, it is relatively rarely argued that multiculturalism as a policy is incompatible per se with integration. Rather, the emphasis is placed on weaknesses in how the policy has been interpreted and implemented in particular contexts. Also treated as open to interpretation is how far society should be prepared to accommodate cultural practices that run counter to its wider norms. While encouraging diversity in relation to, for example, music and cuisine clearly enriches any society and is undemanding, difficulties have arisen even in relation to relatively mundane issues such as dress, as controversies in a number of countries over the veil and the headscarf in the case of Muslims have underlined. Marriage practices provide a further area in which there is tension between the norms of a particular religion and those of the wider society, as embodied in the civil law.

While debate on these issues may generate considerable heat, precisely how the balance is struck is generally of no great political significance. For the most part, policies in these areas have relatively little impact on the lives of the overwhelming majority of people living in the countries concerned. Commonly the people affected are immigrants whose political influence is slight and who in any event rarely constitute a cohesive political force. Thus, while there has been considerable scare-mongering over the size of the Muslim minority in a number of European countries, there is little basis for imagining that there is any unity of purpose among Muslim immigrants on the controversies that have arisen over such matters as wearing the headscarf, blasphemy laws and the status of women. Indeed, the evidence is entirely to the contrary, with sharp divisions of opinion on these issues within such communities (Cassidy 2005). From the perspective of national politics, there appears to be relatively little at stake in how such controversies are resolved in most ordinary liberal democracies and, perhaps partly for that reason, there is considerable variation in the policies of different countries. That might seem to mean that these issues would have relatively little resonance for the politics of deeply divided societies.

Civil Rights

The one case where the political stability of a well established liberal democracy was at stake was the United States in the 1960s, when the demands for integration by the civil rights movement headed by Martin Luther King presented a challenge to the governance of the country that

had the potential for creating widespread disorder. The American movement's success in bringing about desegregation in the Deep South was an
inspiration for people in other societies, including deeply divided ones. In
particular, the Northern Ireland civil rights movement consciously based
itself on the American example, not just in the methods it employed but
also in the integrationist goals it pursued. Frank Wright compared the two
cases in his seminal study of Northern Ireland. He noted that both movements depended on intervention by the central government.

> In both cases they sought meaningful equality of citizen rights in the hope
> that this would create a more harmonious relationship with the dominant
> majorities, both Protestant and white. Crucial to the success of both was
> drawing the metropolitan power into the regional situations and obliging it
> to act in a reconstructive manner. The past pattern, in which dominant
> society defiance actions had shaped the totality of relationships, had to be
> broken.
>   Necessarily, civil rights strategy had to operate on integrationist princi-
> ples, even if these were only implicit, and build up (while transforming the
> character of) the authority of the metropolitan state in opposition to the local
> system of rule of the dominant bloc. (Wright 1987: 164)

However, the outcome of the two movements was very different: the
passage of civil rights legislation and the ending of legally enforced segregation and discrimination in the American case, and a quarter of a
century of violent conflict in the case of Northern Ireland. The starkness
of the difference makes it worthwhile considering why the American
movement was so much more successful than its Northern Ireland coun-
terpart. Admittedly, the achievements of the American movement should
not be overstated. It secured an end to the most overt manifestations of
racism, but, in socio-economic terms, large inequalities remain along racial
lines. And, politically, race is still an important determinant of voting
behaviour, especially in the Deep South, notwithstanding Obama's election
as President in 2008. But these qualifications do not override the success
of integration in the American case. The complete failure of this strategy
in Northern Ireland is underlined by the fact that the peace process of
the 1990s was based on a radically different framework from that of
integration.
    Neither Northern Ireland nor the Deep South was independent. Both
were part of larger political entities, yet both were sufficiently different,
during the era of their civil rights movements, from the countries of which
they were part, to be describable as separate societies. Northern Ireland is
the clearer case, as it had its own government. The Deep South was more
fully integrated into the American political system and there was little

realistic prospect of the subordinate community achieving what the dominant community in this region had failed to achieve in the nineteenth century – separation from the rest of the country. While there were black nationalists in the African American community during the 1960s, their influence was marginal compared to the influence of Irish nationalism among Northern Ireland's Catholic population. It was much easier for Protestants and unionists to portray the Northern Ireland civil rights movement as a Trojan horse for Irish nationalists than it was for Southern segregationists to persuade Americans that the civil rights movement there had communist inspiration.

Both movements faced violence from opponents, but the American movement was more successful in sustaining support for a strategy of non-violence in the face of this provocation. This in part reflected the fact that African Americans stood to gain far more from simple legal reforms to their position than did Catholics in Northern Ireland. To put the point another way, the level of oppression of Catholics in Northern Ireland was by no means on a par with that of African Americans. This also meant that there was less ground for unionist leaders to concede, though it should be stressed that the debate has been on how much discrimination Catholics were subjected to under unionist rule, not on whether there was discrimination (Whyte 1983). The unionist prime minister of Northern Ireland during the height of the civil rights movement was Terence O'Neill. O'Neill was a reformer, and it briefly seemed in December 1968 that his positive response to the demands of the civil rights movement, admittedly under pressure from the British government, would defuse the growing crisis. O'Neill resigned four months later due to divisions in his party and following a security scare as a result of bomb explosions wrongly attributed to the Irish Republican Army but perpetrated by Protestants to undermine the prime minister.

In the aftermath of his resignation, O'Neill gave an interview to the *Belfast Telegraph* that was widely quoted by nationalists to justify their contention that an integrationist solution within the existing constitutional framework was not feasible, given unionist attitudes towards the minority. O'Neill asserted:

> It is frightfully hard to explain to Protestants that if you give Roman Catholics a good job and a good house they will live like Protestants, because they will see neighbours with cars and television sets. They will refuse to have 18 children. But if a Roman Catholic is jobless and lives in a most ghastly hovel, he will rear 18 children on national assistance. If you treat Roman Catholics with due consideration and kindness they will live like Protestants, in spite of the authoritarian nature of their church. (Quoted in Bew and Gillespie 1999: 16)

Many nationalists saw these patronising comments as evidence that the aim of even a reformer such as O'Neill was assimilation rather than integration.

Generally speaking, the term 'deeply divided society' is applied to independent states, though there are some examples of its being applied to a region of a state, and the outstanding example in this context is Northern Ireland. Indeed Northern Ireland is one of the most common examples in the literature of a deeply divided society, if not the most common. It might seem reasonable to apply the concept to other cases with which Northern Ireland is frequently compared. On this basis it might be considered appropriate to apply it to the American case. However, there are some difficulties in doing so. Should the term be applied to the whole of the South or simply to the Deep South? If the latter, how precisely should the region be delineated? From the perspective of political institutions, individual states might seem the most relevant category. Yet to single out particular states as individual examples of deeply divided societies detracts from their similar trajectory. The simplest answer might be to use the original states of the Confederacy as a starting point.

But, however these complications are addressed, the American case does provide an arguable basis for the contention that it is possible for a deeply divided society to be profoundly changed through a process of integration. At the same time it should be acknowledged that the states of the Deep South, and of the South more generally, have not totally shed the effects of the years of segregation. Informal segregation is widespread in the region. Politically, the voting behaviour of the South differs from the rest of the country, and that is even more marked in the case of the Deep South. This was most clearly reflected in the outcome of the 2008 presidential election in the United States. Whereas Obama won the votes of very nearly half of whites in states outside the South, his share of the white vote across the South was 30 per cent. It was even lower in the states of the Deep South. Thus, in the Deep South state of Mississippi, Obama won only 11 per cent of the white vote, which ensured that Obama failed to carry the state with the largest proportion of African American voters in the country. In Alabama, Obama won only 10 per cent of the white vote (Jenkins 2009).

Another difficulty in using the American case to support the proposition that integration might be a viable strategy for the transformation of other deeply divided societies is that it is difficult to maintain that the civil rights movement under Martin Luther King challenged the political legitimacy of the American system. On the contrary, he used federal institutions and, most particularly, the Supreme Court to force change on the power-holders at the state level. And if the extent of the states' political integration within the federal system is used to make the argument that the whole of the United States should form the basis of comparison of the American case with other polities, it might seem more appropriate to place it in the category of moderately divided societies, a feature of which is political parties drawing support across potential fault lines that help to prevent the political institutionalisation of such divisions. This is, after all, a role that has been played successfully by the Democratic Party in the United States. Another example of a political party that has helped to transcend racial and ethnic divisions is the British Labour Party; and many other examples might be cited.

Non-Racialism

But, leaving aside the progress of racial integration in the United States, there is in any event another case that might be used to demonstrate the viability of integration as a strategy for transforming a deeply divided society, and that is South Africa's transition from apartheid to a non-racial democracy. Throughout the Cold War South Africa was a byword for racism, and after the decolonisation of the European empires and desegregation in the United States apartheid seemed an anachronism. However, there seemed very little prospect that the white minority would voluntarily give up power. There were concerns from an early date that the demise of apartheid would be accompanied by a racial bloodbath, particularly if whites believed that the only alternative to apartheid was (African) majority rule. In the light of the argument that deeply divided societies required special forms of governance, it was a short step to contending that South Africa, as a deeply divided society, was a prime case for the adoption of power-sharing or consociational alternatives to majoritarianism. But there was a powerful counter-argument. This was that the effect of special provisions for minorities in the political realm would be to entrench the socio-economic inequalities along racial lines that had developed under apartheid. And there was the implication that such a system would lack legitimacy and consequently perpetuate political instability.

When President de Klerk launched South Africa's transition in February 1990 by releasing Nelson Mandela from jail and lifting the ban on the African National Congress (ANC), this amounted to an acknowledgement not just that apartheid had failed but that putting a new system into place would require negotiations with a range of political organisations, including the ANC. But it was President de Klerk's intention that group rights would be a fundamental feature of any new dispensation his party agreed to in the course of negotiations. The National Party's objective was that power-sharing among the parties would form part of the constitution of the new South Africa. But, because that would have entrenched white privileges, it was opposed by the ANC. National Party negotiators were well versed in the literature on consociationalism that underscored the need for special mechanisms to protect minorities in deeply divided societies, so were well equipped to make that case. However, they were unable to secure international support for their argument, with the American government in particular making clear its unwillingness to support the principle that group rights should be constitutionally protected.

The conflict between the government and the ANC over the issue led to an impasse in the negotiations in May 1992. At the same time, the high level of political violence compounded fears that the situation could spiral out of control (as shown in Table 4.3 in Chapter 4). The government had initially hoped that the violence would weaken the position of the ANC, but it became evident during the course of 1992 that it was having an adverse effect on support for the National Party. The government then gave ground, giving priority to achieving an agreement with the ANC. It abandoned its aim of entrenching group rights in return for what were dubbed 'sunset clauses'. These were time-limited provisions for power-sharing that gave positions in a government of national unity to parties that gained over 5 per cent of the vote in the country's democratic elections in April 1994, but with no right to any veto over the majority in the government over policy. This was a very watered down version of power-sharing for a temporary period.

Nonetheless, some advocates of consociationalism, including Arend Lijphart himself, hailed the outcome of the South African transition as a triumph for the consociational idea (Lijphart 1994: 222). However, others, most notably Hermann Giliomee, bitterly attacked de Klerk precisely for his failure to have prevented majority rule (Giliomee 2003: 643). As had already been foreshadowed by the outcome of the negotiations of 1993, the final constitution that came into force in 1997 made no provision for power-sharing. By this time the National Party had already resigned from the government of national unity, preferring opposition to occupying cabinet positions for another few years, but without much influence on the government's policies. Landslide victories by the ANC in the general elections of 1994, 1999, 2004 and 2009 have underscored ANC domination of the political system. The ANC secured well over 60 per cent of the vote in each of the elections, as underlined in Table 5.1.

Even a split within the ANC's ranks prior to the elections of 2009, leading to the formation of the Congress of the People, made only a minor dent in its level of support. The prospect that the ANC's hegemony will continue is underpinned by the polarisation of the electorate on racial lines,

Table 5.1   Top three parties in terms of share of the vote in South African national elections since the transition to democracy, highlighting ANC's dominance

1994	1999	2004	2009
African National Congress 62.65%	African National Congress 66.25%	African National Congress 69.69%	African National Congress 65.90%
National Party 20.39%	Democratic Party 9.56%	Democratic Alliance 12.37%	Democratic Alliance 16.66%
Inkatha Freedom Party 10.54%	Inkatha Freedom Party 8.58%	Inkatha Freedom Party 6.97%	Congress of the People 7.42%

SOURCE Compiled from figures on the website of the Independent Electoral Commission at http://www.elections.org.za/

though the overlap between race and differences in income and wealth, as well as responses to opinion surveys, provide grounds for arguing that voters are not motivated by race in their choice of party. At the same time, dissatisfaction among the ANC's supporters over the delivery of services by government has sustained opponents of the ANC in the belief that its domination of the political system will eventually be brought to an end by the electorate.

But what is striking about the South African case is that both the ANC and the main opposition party, the Democratic Alliance, have couched their appeal to voters in non-racial terms, and in their leadership and member-ship reflect the 'rainbow nation', as it has been dubbed. Further, despite the intensity of the opposition's criticism of the ANC's stewardship of the country, there has been very little questioning of the legitimacy of the system. Thus, it is widely accepted that South Africa has remained a fully functioning constitutional democracy since the completion of South Africa's transition from apartheid in 1994. The achievement of racial inte-gration in the political realm has been accompanied by social integration. This has largely been through the rapid rise of an African elite and middle class that have moved into the formerly white suburbs of the country's cities under apartheid. The result has been that at its upper and middle levels the society is racially integrated. There is little racial integration among the poor and unemployed, as they come overwhelmingly from the African majority.

Alternative lines of argument are possible at this point. Each of these has large implications for the analysis of and prescriptions for deeply divided societies. The first is that special mechanisms to safeguard minorities are not in fact needed to sustain constitutional democracy in a deeply divided society and that the alternative approach of seeking to erode divisions through integration is possible. Further, since a common criticism of approaches such as consociationalism is that they tend to entrench existing divisions, it might be argued that the South African example shows that there is not merely an alternative, but one that is superior in terms of the evolution of the society in the long term. The second line of argument is that, with the dismantlement of apartheid, South Africa ceased to be a deeply divided society. Evidence for this argument is the absence of a serious challenge to the legitimacy of the system that has been established in South Africa under the country's 1997 constitution. Murray and Simeon conclude their analysis of the position of minorities in post-apartheid South Africa as follows:

> Complaints that the new majority South Africa government discriminates against its minorities remain a common part of South African political discourse [. . .] But what is most striking is not the intensity of these debates but, rather, the lack of intensity. There is no suggestion that the African majority is riven by internal linguistic and ethnic differences. There is no suggestion of systematic exclusion or repression of minorities by the majority. (Murray and Simeon 2008: 434–5)

However, it might still be argued that it is too early to conclude that the current system will prove durable in the long run. An important test of majoritarian democratic systems is whether alternation of power is possible through the ballot box. In particular, will the ANC be willing to abide by the results of an election in which it is voted out of office?

The implications of each of these lines of argument are worth considering. In particular, why was it unnecessary in South Africa's case to make special provision for minorities in its post-transition constitution? The obvious answer is that the minorities that might have been accorded group rights were substantially better off in terms of both income and wealth than the African majority. While the Inkatha Freedom Party secured substantial support among the rural Zulu population on an ethno-nationalist platform, there was otherwise very little support for ethnically based political parties among the African majority. The priority for the majority was ending racial discrimination, and the ANC, in its espousing of non-racialism and the objective of 'one person, one vote' in a unitary state, was best placed to represent the interests of the majority. Further, the higher levels of education of the minorities and their ability to compete in domestic and global markets placed the minorities in a strong position to continue to enjoy higher incomes than the majority, notwithstanding the ending of racial discrimination and the enactment of measures to assist what were dubbed 'historically disadvantaged groups'. While coloureds and Indians fell into the category of groups that had suffered discrimination in the past, they had not been subject to the same degree of discrimination as Africans. In particular, neither coloureds nor Indians had been subject to the pass laws that controlled influx into the urban areas. The difference was reflected in political divisions within both groups and less support for the ANC within these groups than among Africans.

In practice, the ANC's desire to create opportunities for upward mobility among those who were previously subjected to racial discrimination has acted as a constraint on the pursuit of policies aimed at the radical redistribution of income and wealth. The restraint shown might have had less legitimacy among the majority if it appeared to result from the existence of minority vetoes or other mechanisms. But it is also possible to argue that the minorities have no guarantee that this restraint will continue to be exercised in the future. The polarisation that took place in the course of the country's 2009 general election in part reflected fears that Jacob Zuma, as a populist ANC leader, might adopt more radical policies than his predecessors in the economic sphere. Yet the consensus that exists on the legitimacy of the political system as a constitutional democracy does set post-transition South Africa apart from most other examples of deeply divided societies. While South Africa faces huge problems, including a very high crime rate, an AIDS pandemic, widespread unemployment and a host of other social problems, these challenges have not raised doubts about the country's political stability. And it is also worth underlining that the cultural diversity of the country has not been put in question by the ANC's emphasis on non-racialism.

Racism as a Special Case

The further question that the South African case and that of desegregation in the United States raise is whether the trajectory that they have followed is available to other deeply divided societies. It is significant that in both cases there was elaborate and formal enforcement of a system of racial domination. Furthermore, the system in each case was justified in terms of an explicitly racist ideology. The global turn against racism affected both. As the policy of an independent state, apartheid survived longer than segregation in a part of the United States. But the illegitimacy of racism meant that, when change came in both places, there was a wholesale repudiation of the old system, even though its legacy left a lasting mark on the distribution of income and wealth in both societies. A further consequence of the illegitimacy of racism was that political claims could not be effectively made on the basis of entrenching the rights of racial groups once the system unravelled.

By contrast, in most other cases of deeply divided societies there remains a conflict over the legitimacy of the polity in which both sides are able to make a case for the primacy of their claim. In particular, it is obviously difficult to adjudicate on competing ethno-nationalist claims on territories that have historically been mixed in ethnic terms. Even if one ethnic group forms a majority within existing boundaries, a minority or minorities may be able to pursue the option of secession. This presupposes predominance of the ethnic group in question in a particular region. The fact that there was no state within the United States in which African Americans constituted a majority precluded that option in the United States, though it was by no means the only reason why separatism enjoyed little support among African Americans. In the case of South Africa, one response among Afrikaner nationalists to the prospect of majority rule was the proposal for the creation of a separate Afrikaner state, but the appeal of this idea proved limited, as it became evident how limited the scope for the establishment of a *volkstaat* would be. The pursuit of either of these options was effectively undercut by the collapse of the general legitimacy of racism, by tainting the notion of the *volkstaat* and by undermining the claim of black separatists about the potency and permanency of white racism that underpinned their case.

Parties supporting integration exist or have existed in many deeply divided societies. Similarly, there are numerous examples of social movements that have been able to transcend the main fault line in these societies on particular issues for limited periods. In particular, in societies not deeply divided on class lines, trade unions commonly champion integration so as to prevent the development of a split labour market, since a divided labour market tends to facilitate the undercutting of wages by employers. Similarly, socialist parties seeking to mobilise on a class basis may try to secure support across the communal divide. But a fundamental characteristic of deeply divided societies places limits in most cases on integration as a means of transforming the society. This is the lack of consensus on the framework for making decisions in deeply divided societies. The success of organisations supporting integration tends to depend on whether they are able to neutralise arguments over the framework for decision-making and thus can avoid calling the legitimacy of the polity into question through their actions. The difficulty is that a comparatively small segment of the society can ensure that the question of the legitimacy of the polity does come to the fore and takes precedence over other issues. The fate of the Northern Ireland civil rights movement, which depended for its success on partition not being in question, illustrates the point.

The proneness of deeply divided societies to political violence reflects the centrality to their politics of contestation over the legitimacy of the existing polity. The absence of political violence in contemporary South Africa is one reason for arguing that the country has ceased to be a deeply divided society. Moderately divided societies are not as vulnerable to political violence on an ongoing basis as are deeply divided ones. And in moderately divided societies integration through involvement in broadly based political parties remains an attractive option for members of minorities who wish to further their interests, whether as individuals or as representatives of their communities, under the existing political framework. Even those, such as regional nationalists, who wish to see changes in the decision-making framework may be content, in the absence of political violence, to pursue their objectives under the existing system.

At the same time the feasibility of political projects – whether to create a classless society, to establish a new nation state or to set up a secular state or a theocracy – depends on a wide range of factors, including regional and international circumstances. And that also applies to the strategy of integration, which also depends on the surrounding circumstances as to whether it is capable of gaining mass support and seems a credible way forward. As Nagle and Clancy point out, '[w]hen ethnonational groups do talk about integration with [a] rival group, it is usually made to rhyme with assimilation' (Nagle and Clancy 2010: 218). The current emphasis on multiculturalism has also tended to undercut the appeal of integration as a way of tackling division in society, even though the two concepts are not necessarily contradictory. A consequence is to direct attention away from how successful the process of integration has been in many societies. The complete opposite of dissolving divisions through integration is the separation of people through the creation of new political entities, and this is the next topic that will be considered.

6 PARTITION AND POPULATION TRANSFER

If integration no longer holds out the hope of dissolving divisions, there remain two other ways in which states or political movements may seek to eliminate divisions. Firstly, the territory may be divided, thereby in effect creating two or more societies through the process of establishing new polities. Secondly, the composition of the polity may be changed through the enforced, or at least incentivised, movement of population. This chapter will largely focus on the first of these ways, namely territorial changes. However, these two possibilities should not be seen as mutually exclusive. Indeed, changes of the boundaries of territories are very commonly accompanied by movement of population, whether brought about directly by actions of the state or simply as the result of insecurity. Changes in boundaries tend to be associated with violent conflict, and most particularly with interstate war. During the Cold War following the Second World War, there were relatively few interstate wars and consequently, despite the revolution in world politics brought about by decolonisation, relatively few territorial changes. The main exceptions were the Korean War and the series of wars involving Israel in the Middle East. The former, which might also be seen as a civil war with external involvement on both sides, ensured the continued partition of the Korean Peninsula; the latter led to changes to boundaries in the Middle East that remain disputed and/or provisional.

The period since the end of the Cold War has witnessed the largest increase in membership of the United Nations since the ending of the colonial era in the 1960s. This wave of state creation has primarily been a product of processes of partition and secession that followed the collapse of communism in Eastern Europe and in the Soviet Union. The disintegration of the Soviet Union in 1991, the break-up of Yugoslavia and the velvet divorce between the Czech Republic and Slovakia have resulted in the creation of a large number of newly independent states, though precedents existed for some of these. In particular, the Baltic states of Estonia, Lithuania and Latvia had been members of the League of Nations. However, as the case of Eritrea's secession from Ethiopia illustrates, the emergence of new states has not entirely been confined to one region of the world. With the emergence of at least two states in Sudan – hitherto Africa's largest state – and with the de facto division of Somalia, the commitment of African states to the acceptance of the boundaries bequeathed by the process of decolonisation may come under further strain.

Fragmentation

In fact events in Eastern Europe have given immense encouragement to secessionist movements in every part of the world. The anathema that the international community had maintained against secession during the Cold War has lost much of its credibility as a consequence of the changes that have been made to state boundaries since 1990. Similarly, the international community's declarations on upholding the territorial integrity of existing states sound increasingly hollow in the light particularly of the change in Western policy towards secession. Paradoxically, the world's further political fragmentation has occurred against the backdrop of globalisation of the world economy and of processes of regional economic integration that have tended to reduce the sovereign state's freedom of action in the economic sphere. At the same time globalisation has facilitated the operation of transnational movements centred on the championing of particular ethnic or religious groups.

However, the trend towards the creation of new polities should not be overstated. Much of the international community remains hostile towards both partition and secession. This stems not merely from the self-interest of existing states in the maintenance of the territorial status quo, but also from a recognition that the contested legitimacy of partition and secession lies at the basis of many of the world's conflicts, whether in the Middle East, South Asia, Africa or Europe. Successful partition or secession, in the sense that the new boundaries created both achieve and retain universal legitimacy, is a rare event. Norway's secession from Sweden in 1905 is an unusual instance, where the new boundaries have achieved acceptance and are uncontested. However, the long-running conflict over the partition of

Ireland is much more typical of the difficulties that are encountered in securing acceptance of new boundaries. Partition and secession are overlapping concepts, though with slightly different connotations. Partition simply refers to the division of a territory. It can be carried out by Great Powers without reference to the wishes of the population, or even the rulers of the existing polity, as in the notorious case of the successive partitions of Poland, beginning with its division among Austria, Prussia and Russia in 1772. That case of course did not involve the creation of new political entities. More commonly these days it does, even when it is the product of the actions of external forces, as in the partitions of Germany, Vietnam and Korea after the Second World War.

Secession in a political context refers to withdrawal from subjection to the authority of an existing state. Because political authority is exercised territorially, successful secession inevitably has territorial implications. Another way of putting that is to say that, when successful, secession results in the partition of an existing political entity. However, movements seeking the independence of a particular region of a country are generally referred to as secessionist or separatist rather than as partitionist, even if, logically speaking, successful secession entails the partition of an existing polity. One reason for this is that secessions are generally seen as unilateral actions and as occurring against the wishes of the existing polity, as in the secession of the Southern states from the United States. Of course, in this particular instance, the result was a civil war, and ultimately the military defeat of the attempt to secede. Two important attempts at secession in the 1960s were the exit of Katanga from the Congo and that of Biafra from Nigeria. In both these cases the secessions were also ultimately defeated. However, in a small number of cases, secessionists have won the civil war that has ensued from their declaration of independence. Bangladesh, with a lot of help from India, successfully broke away from Pakistan in 1971 (Heraclides 1991: 147–64). Until 1991 this was the only example of a secessionist victory in such a situation, when both Slovenia and Croatia succeeded in exiting from Yugoslavia.

Slightly different from either of these cases is the situation where secession/partition takes place by mutual agreement, at least of the political elites. If cases such as the dissolution of loose unions like that between Egypt and Syria to form the United Arab Republic are discounted, the most important such instance prior to the end of the Cold War was Singapore's departure from the Malaysian Federation. There have been three important cases since the end of the Cold War: the division of Czechoslovakia into the Czech Republic and Slovakia; Eritrea's departure from Ethiopia; and the third occurring as a result of the vote in favour of independence in Southern Sudan in January 2011. The contrast between the procedures followed in the first two cases was striking. The political leaders who decided on the dissolution of Czechoslovakia, to the distress of many people, including the country's president, proceeded with the partition without consulting the people in a referendum. Surveys at the time indicated that majorities of both Czechs and Slovaks opposed the split (Havlová 2005: 112). The creation of the country in the first place, at the end of the First World War, had been brought about similarly by the actions of political elites; this makes Czechoslovakia a country that came into existence, and then disappeared, without popular endorsement of either event (Leff 1996). The overthrow of the military dictatorship in Ethiopia by a coalition of different secessionist movements and opposition groups created a favourable political context for Eritrea's secession. Nonetheless, the political elites in this instance decided to seek – and achieved – popular endorsement for the process at each appropriate juncture. Yet, ironically, it was the Eritrean–Ethiopian case that led to violent conflict: a war between the two states over a frontier dispute (Fisher 1999).

Secession is very often not the first choice either of a disaffected community or of a minority fearful of majority rule within existing boundaries – whether because of the extension of the franchise or decolonisation. This is because the pursuit of secession is often neither a feasible nor an attractive option, given the spatial distribution of the community or the minority within the polity. However, if the political leaders of large communities remain at loggerheads, partition may be seen as an alternative to severe inter-communal conflict, and even civil war. That is what happened in British India on the eve of independence, resulting in the creation of two states, India and Pakistan. But partition proved painful and left 'unfinished business' (Kumar 2005: 2). Disputed boundaries, the secession of Bangladesh and conflict over the status of Kashmir have been the cause of a series of wars between the two countries.

Somewhat similarly, the seeds of the partition of Cyprus lay in conflict between the island's main communities during the last years of British colonial rule. In this case, partition had long formed an objective of leaders of the Turkish Cypriot community (Richmond 1998: 73). But it should be noted that partition was not brought about directly by fighting between the communities, but by the military intervention of an external power, Turkey, 14 years after independence. While the partition of Cyprus halted violence between the Greek Cypriot and the Turkish Cypriot communities virtually completely, it has not ended the dispute. In particular, only Turkey ever accorded recognition to the Turkish Republic of North Cyprus. At the time of Cyprus's accession to the European Union it had seemed that a formula had been found for reunification. Ironically, the deal was voted down by Greek Cypriots, while it was supported by Turkish Cypriots. The situation in Bosnia-Herzegovina is another instance where the separation of communities has been an outcome of civil war, one influenced and affected by external parties, as civil wars often are. But in this case NATO and the EU have acted to prevent partition.

Absorption and Irredentism

From an historical perspective, a more important source of changes in international boundaries than partition or secession has been the process of absorption of small states by great powers. Indeed, the era of the operation of the European balance of power system, up to its destruction by the First World War, saw a large reduction in the number of European states. By contrast, the international political system since 1945 has seen a large expansion in the number of states. However, against the main trend, there have been a few cases of the union of two independent states into one. The unification of Tanganyika and Zanzibar to form Tanzania is one example. The political context of the union was a revolution in Zanzibar shortly after the islands achieved independence in December 1963. The revolution was directed against the Arab minority that had hitherto ruled over the islands. It prompted a chain reaction of instability through East Africa. This made the restoration of political stability in Zanzibar a priority for Tanganyika, providing the basis for an alliance between the mainland and political leaders in the islands that was cemented through union of the two states in April 1964. Under the union, Zanzibar has enjoyed a large measure of autonomy, having its own president and parliament. Nonetheless, political divisions in the islands continue to reflect differences on the relationship with the mainland. There is some support for the restoration of the islands' independence in what has been historically the main opposition party, though the party is now part of a power-sharing arrangement.

The unification of North and South Yemen followed the end of the Cold War. A Marxist government had existed in the South. Unification meant the inclusion in Yemen of the port of Aden, which had once been ruled as part of British India, then as a colony before British withdrawal in 1967. The disorderly nature of the withdrawal, including a failure to put in place political institutions to take over the colony, had an impact on the thinking of the founders of the Provisional Irish Republican Army, who believed that it set a precedent for their securing a British declaration of intent to withdraw from Northern Ireland (McGuire 1973). With unification, the longstanding leader of North Yemen, Ali Abdullah Saleh, became the president of the united country. He retained his grip on power for the next twenty years, despite numerous crises. In 1994 the South attempted to secede, and there was a brief civil war before the authority of the central government was re-imposed on Aden. President Saleh presented himself as an ally in America's global war on terror, but the country became, nonetheless, a base for al Qaeda. In 2011 Yemen became engulfed in the Arab Spring, forcing concessions from President Saleh. One may add to Tanzania and Yemen the marginally different cases of the reunification of Vietnam following the communist victory in the long-running civil war in South Vietnam in 1975 and of the reunification of Germany in 1990 following the coming down of the Berlin Wall.

Another potential source of changes in boundaries is irredentism. The origin of this term in the Latin *redimere* (meaning 'to ransom', 'release', redeem', whence the Italian *irredento*, 'unredeemed') reflects the ambition to recover lost territory. But it is now commonly applied to any situation in which a state seeks to expand its boundaries by incorporating part of the territory of a neighbouring state to which it lays claim, whether on historical grounds or because of ethnic affinity with people in the region in question. For example, during the 1970s Somalia championed the rights of Somalis in the Ogaden region of Ethiopia to secede from Ethiopia and to join Somalia, and this culminated in a war between the two states in 1977 and 1978 in which Somalia was defeated (Chazan *et al.* 1992: 347–9). In cases where an ethnic group straddles an international boundary, the pressure for a change in the boundary so as to unite or reunite the ethnic group often comes from the ethnic group itself rather than from one of the affected states. Thus the aspiration of nationalists in Northern Ireland to a united Ireland has been stronger than that of the Irish state itself, at least since the start of Northern Ireland's troubles in 1968. Calculation of the impact of irredentism on its relations with other states is a strongly restraining influence on state behaviour, since irredentism is viewed with even greater disfavour by the international community than is secessionism.

Contested boundaries are one reason why a government may lack legitimacy in the eyes of the inhabitants of the territory it rules over or in the eyes of the international community – or both. It is one of the most difficult problems to resolve. The League of Nations tried plebiscites in disputed areas. However, that was in the context of settling the boundaries of new states in the wake of a major cataclysm. Most states would strongly resist the notion that their boundaries could be constantly put in question in this way. Of course, the nature of government is also a significant factor in whether a particular regime is perceived as legitimate internally and externally. Since the end of the Cold War, liberal democracy has become the predominant form of government, so much so that there tends to be a presumption that democratic regimes are legitimate while non-democratic regimes are not. This almost certainly overstates the compatibility between liberal democracy and stable and effective government in countries with very low living standards, while also underestimating the capacity of forms of government that diverge from the principles of liberal democracy to generate popular support through providing security and stability. However, from an international perspective, being a liberal democracy does tend to be seen these days as an important criterion of a regime's legitimacy. Admittedly, in practice there is considerable variation in the quality of governance under different liberal democracies, and the outward form is not always a reliable guide to the effectiveness of political institutions in particular cases.

To function effectively, liberal democracy requires a broad domestic consensus on the framework for decision-making. While referenda and elections may play a part in establishing acceptance of such a framework, it is a mistake to treat these simply as part of the functioning of liberal democracy, since plainly the principles of liberal democracy, just by themselves, provide little guide as to what the boundaries of any state should be. Furthermore, a referendum or other form of popular vote may not be successful in creating the basis for a consensus on future decision-making. For example, the 1973 border poll in Northern Ireland did not reconcile nationalists to partition (Bew and Gillespie 1999: 60). The notion of democratic secession begs the question of who has the right to determine the boundaries of the region that seeks to depart from the existing polity. Further, what rights does the rest of society have in the case of secession, since the balance of political forces may well be affected by it? Even in cases where secession enjoys overwhelming support in a relatively homogeneous region, as in the case of Slovenia's withdrawal from Yugoslavia in 1991, it could be argued that consideration should be given not just to the exiting region's prospects of sustaining legitimate political institutions and achieving prosperity for its citizens, but also to the impact of its departure on the rest of the country. Thus, in the particular case of Slovenia, its departure from Yugoslavia was a catalyst for further and far more destabilising division (Glenny 1992: 96–7). In short, the departure of one region from a country may prompt further 'sequential secessions' (Pavković with Radan 2007: 129).

But the issue most salient to the analysis of deeply divided societies is that an almost inevitable consequence of changes in boundaries, unless (and sometimes even if) accompanied by movement of population, is the creation of new minorities. Furthermore, the fact that these minorities are created in circumstances in which the boundaries may still be disputed provides potent conditions for the emergence or reinforcement of deeply divided societies. Whether a deeply divided society is the outcome also depends on a number of other factors, including the size of the potentially disaffected minority, its transnational connections and the attitude of other states. Minorities trapped in new states they do not wish to be part of can seek to secede, either to rejoin the entity from which the new state came or to form an entirely new state – a process that has been dubbed 'recursive secession' (Pavković with Radan 2007: 129). Examples of recursive secession include the cases of Abkhazia and South Ossetia, which broke away from Georgia. A key factor in sustaining their de facto independence has been the support of Russia. In 2008 this support proved decisive in preventing Georgia from reincorporating South Ossetia by military force. The Serbs in the Krajina region of Croatia also sought to escape incorporation into the new independent state during Croatia's secession from Yugoslavia in the early 1990s, but their attempt at recursive secession failed. After this failure, many Serbs were driven out of Croatia in a process of ethnic cleansing that quite commonly follows secession. Expulsions of minorities may be argued by separatist movements during the course of secession to be necessary to secure the borders of the new entity, or, after the event, to be justified by the minority's disloyalty to the new state.

Partition of Ireland

Partition looms large in the story of some of the world's most renowned or notorious deeply divided societies. Though the Northern Ireland problem can be conceptualised in various ways, the commonest is as the partition of the island of Ireland by the British government under the 1920 Government of Ireland Act. But an equally legitimate way of conceptualising the problem is as the partition of the British Isles, since at the point of partition the whole of Ireland was an integral part of the larger British political system. However, because partition was a response to the existence of a popular movement in Catholic Ireland for independence from Britain, it might also be seen in terms of the secession from Britain of the 26 counties that were to make up the Irish state. Finally, since Northern Ireland was required to opt out of the arrangements that were finally agreed between the British government and Irish nationalists in 1921 if Northern Ireland was to remain in existence, partition might arguably be looked upon as the secession of the six counties of the north-east from the Irish state, in other words as a case of recursive secession. Thus, for the brief moment in time between the establishment of the Irish state and the exercise of its opt-out by the government in Northern Ireland, a united Ireland existed in theory. But, however the genesis of the Northern Irish problem is conceptualised, another important consideration is that the sharp communal division between Protestants and Catholics in the north-east of the island predated partition.

Consequently, it is facile to attribute all the ills of the society in Northern Ireland to partition, or to see the solution to all its ills in Irish unity. Further, one might argue that, from the perspective of the other political entities affected by partition, Britain and the Republic of Ireland, partition was stabilising. Nevertheless, it is evident that partition worsened relations between Protestants and Catholics in Northern Ireland, deepening the communal divide between them. At the onset of Northern Ireland's troubles in the late 1960s, it quickly became apparent that much of world opinion saw partition as illegitimate and regarded the outcome of a united Ireland as inevitable in much the same way as majority rule in Southern Africa was regarded as inevitable. In short, unionists appeared to the outside world as swimming against the tide of history. There were a number of reasons for these perceptions. The emphasis placed by the international community on territorial integrity as a norm made the partition of an island particularly problematic. Only a handful of islands in the world are split between different sovereign states, and where islands have been divided as a result of inter-communal conflict this has proved highly controversial, as the world's unwillingness to legitimise the partition of Cyprus underlines. Unusually, in the case of East Timor the international community did favour the re-establishment of the division of an island. The explanation is that Indonesia's annexation of East Timor in 1975 violated another important norm of the international community, the principle established during the period of decolonisation that colonies were entitled to independence within the boundaries that had been established by the colonial powers. Admittedly, during the Cold War strategic considerations overrode the commitment of the major Western powers to this principle in the case of East Timor.

Another reason why international opinion looked askance at Northern Ireland as a political entity was its conditional status. The official position of the British government was that Northern Ireland's membership of the United Kingdom was conditional on that continuing to be the wish of a majority of its electorate, a condition that did not apply to any other part of the United Kingdom. That made Northern Ireland's status appear semi-colonial. Further, the Britishness of the province's Protestants appeared open to question, both because their cultural traditions were so alien to those prevailing on the mainland of the United Kingdom and because of the readiness of Ulster Protestants to defy British governments and the law, in defence of the maintenance of their hegemony. At the time of the onset of the troubles, their attitude appeared to be somewhat similar to that of whites in the Southern states of the United States who had resisted desegregation. In the 1990s perceptions of the Northern Ireland conflict were increasingly influenced by the outbreak of ethnic conflicts in Eastern Europe and the former Soviet Union. The interpretation of the problem in ethnic terms helped to ensure a favourable reception for the Belfast Agreement, with its attempt to accommodate the national identities of both communities through innovative connections among different levels of government across Britain and Ireland. In fact, despite the problems that have been encountered in implementing the Agreement, it continues to be cited as a model for the resolution of ethnic conflicts elsewhere.

However, this has not entirely altered the view, outside of Britain and Ireland, of partition as not fully legitimate and as temporary. The Belfast Agreement provides for the holding of a referendum on the issue of Irish unity, should the Secretary of State for Northern Ireland think it likely that there would be a majority in favour. But, should the vote go against a united Ireland, the Agreement provides for a gap of at least seven years before there is another poll on the issue. The existence of these provisions in the Agreement, as well as the substantial increase in the Catholic proportion of the population of Northern Ireland during the course of the troubles, might suggest that the Agreement was underpinned by the assumption of a coming Catholic and nationalist majority that would end partition. Such an interpretation would make it easier to understand why Catholics voted overwhelmingly in favour of the Agreement and Protestants were equally divided in their response in the referendum. In fact, this view is wide of the mark for a number of reasons.

Firstly, the position that the British government would support Irish unity if there were a majority in Northern Ireland in favour of such a course is not a new position. Not merely has it been a part of previous agreements that British governments have entered into with the Irish governments; it is a logical corollary of the province's conditional membership of the United Kingdom. What is perhaps new is the Agreement's implicit ruling out of any option other than Irish unity or British rule within the terms of the Agreement. Secondly, much more significant is the fact that, under the Agreement, Articles 2 and 3 of the Irish constitution have been re-written to incorporate what is commonly referred to as the principle of consent. The new articles, which came into effect on implementation of the Agreement, provide that a united Ireland can only come about with the consent of majorities in both jurisdictions in Ireland. Though Irish governments have in the past committed themselves to this principle of consent, changing the constitution is a step further. In legal terms, the agreement in 1925 between Northern Ireland and the Irish Free State to uphold the existing border between the two jurisdictions represented Southern acceptance of partition, but that acceptance lacked political legitimacy in so far as it could be presented as forced on the Irish government by the unsatisfactory outcome of the Boundary Commission. However, the endorsement of the changes to Articles 2 and 3 in the Southern referendum on the Belfast Agreement in 1998 clearly did represent full-hearted consent for the continuance of partition under the terms of the Agreement.

Thirdly, nationalist enthusiasm for the Belfast Agreement did not stem simply from expectations that it might lead one day to a united Ireland. The Agreement's provisions for power-sharing, the promise of reform in the fields of justice and policing, the commitment to an equality agenda and the Irish dimension in the form of cross-border bodies were features that appealed to nationalists. The demographic factor was important in this context, not solely because of a belief in a coming Catholic majority but because the narrowing of the difference in the size of the two communities in Northern Ireland enhanced Catholic confidence that political institutions in Northern Ireland would reflect their interests and concerns more fully. Fourthly, the Agreement would not have secured a narrow majority among Protestants if Unionists had believed that it represented a slippery slope to a united Ireland.

Admittedly, unionist acceptance of the Belfast Agreement was based in part on the fear that rejection of the Agreement would be damaging to the interests of unionists because it might impel the British and Irish governments to take steps in the direction of joint sovereignty. And implementation of the Agreement has proved difficult and contested. It has led to a polarisation of opinion that has resulted in the dominance of radical parties on either side of the province's sectarian divide. It took until 2010 for full implementation of the settlement to take place, and then only after two further accords, the St Andrews Agreement of October 2006 and the Hillsborough Agreement of February 2010. While unionists hope that the settlement will provide a framework for the normalisation of partition, the hopes of nationalists remain that it will enable them to realise their aspiration for a united Ireland. Sustaining this ambiguity remains crucial to the settlement's success. Were it to break down, the British and Irish governments would be forced to consider other options.

Among the options likely to be considered by the two governments in the last resort, if the Belfast Agreement could not be restored after a period of suspension, would be repartition. Thus it is possible to argue that partition per se was not a mistake, given the strength of antagonism between Protestants and Catholics on the island of Ireland, but that what went wrong was the incorporation of a large Catholic minority within Northern Ireland. However, it is worth pointing out in this context that the other side of the coin of where the border was drawn was that the Irish Free State was relatively homogeneous. Even that did not prevent serious sectarian violence in the Southern part of Ireland during the course of the War of Independence (Hart 1998). Somewhat paradoxically, such violence came to an end partly as a result of the civil war between nationalists in the Irish Free State over the Anglo-Irish Treaty. But leaving aside the argument as to whether more stable conditions could have been created in the 1920s if Fermanagh and Tyrone, counties with nationalist majorities, had been permitted to join the Irish Free State, it might still be argued that separation of the two communities is the only option left for preventing conflict, given the failure of attempts at political accommodation between the communities.

The objection to repartition in Northern Ireland, as it is to partition in many other cases, is that it is impossible to draw any boundary that does not create new minorities and that the objective of homogeneous blocks of territory could only be achieved through substantial and involuntary movement of population. There is a precedent for mutually agreed movement of population to achieve greater homogeneity, and this is the exchange of population that took place between Turkey and Greece after the First World War. However, apart from this case, this is not a course of action that liberal–democratic governments have been willing to defend as an acceptable policy. Admittedly, in practice, the West as the standard bearer of liberal democracy has not been consistent in opposition to mass expulsions that have arisen in the context of civil wars. But acquiescence in some instances of ethnic cleansing is a reflection of the priority given to strategic interests in the conduct of foreign policy and does not alter the fact that population movement involving any element of compulsion is generally seen as being contrary to liberal–democratic principles.

There are a number of reasons for the attitudes adopted by liberal–democratic governments on this question. In the first place, while it would be possible to persuade some people to move through offering them generous compensation to resettle, the governments would be faced either with being a party to the direct coercion of others to move or with having to take on the responsibility of protecting them if they were allowed to remain. In the second place, most liberal democracies themselves rule over ethnically, racially and religiously diverse populations and do not wish to promote the notion that the existence of diversity should be viewed as a barrier to stable government. In the third place, it is recognised that in any event the return of people to their old homes is difficult to prevent, given countries' international obligations. For example, controls on the movement of people between Northern Ireland and the Republic of Ireland would obviously fall foul of the obligations arising from Britain's and Ireland's membership of the European Union.

The Palestinian Case

The fact that laws barring refugees from returning to the towns and villages they fled from in the course of violent conflict lack international legitimacy has proved a problem both for the Turkish Republic of Northern Cyprus and for the Israeli state. In the case of Cyprus, the demand of Greek Cypriots that the refugees driven out of the northern part of the island by Turkey's invasion in 1974 should be allowed to return to their homes, as a fundamental human right, has been a factor in undercutting efforts to solve the Cyprus problem on the basis of the formula, long favoured by the international community, of a bi-communal, bi-zonal federation. Over every effort to resolve the conflict between Israel and the Palestinians looms the issue of the refugees and their rights to return to areas that their forebears once lived in. If the international community has proved less responsive to the claims of the refugees in this case, it is partly because of the role that the United Nations played in sanctioning partition as a solution to the conflicting political demands of the communities in Palestine after the Second World War. It also partly reflects the very special context in which Israel came into being. Thus Robert Fisk's book on the civil war in Lebanon opens with chapters on the Holocaust and on the keys to houses in Jaffa held by Palestinian refugees in Lebanon as a way of underlining the strength of the competing claims underlying conflict in the Middle East (Fisk 1990: 1–47).

Partition of Palestine was first proposed by the Royal Commission set up by the British government to inquire into the causes of the Arab revolt in 1936. Palestinian hostility towards the Peel Commission's recommendations prompted the British government to abandon the idea of partition and to put in its place the aim of creating a bi-national state. After the Second World War, Britain granted independence to Transjordan, a part of the mandate that had been separately administered virtually from the outset of its establishment. Faced with hostility from both communities in Palestine, Britain opted to hand over responsibility for the territory to the United Nations (UN) as the successor to the League of Nations. The United Nations General Assembly set up a Special Committee on Palestine to make recommendations for the future governance of the area. It proposed that, on termination of the mandate, the territory should be partitioned into an independent Arab state and an independent Jewish state; Jerusalem and its environs were excluded from both states and were to be administered by the Trusteeship Committee of the United Nations. Despite Arab opposition, this partition plan was endorsed by the General Assembly in November 1947.

Israel's declaration of independence coincided with British withdrawal from Palestine in May 1948 and was followed by war between Israel and the neighbouring Arab states, the outcome of which effectively determined the boundaries of the new state. These were appreciably larger than those under the UN partition plan, as well as including a large part of Jerusalem. Further, no independent Arab state was created. Territory on the West Bank of the Jordan River was absorbed into Jordan, while Egypt took over the administration of the Gaza Strip. Both these areas came under Israeli control following the Six-Day War in 1967. The reaction of the United Nations Security Council was to call for 'withdrawal of Israel armed forces from territories occupied in the recent conflict' as part of an overall political settlement. The effect was to undermine the legitimacy of any notions of a greater Israel, while at the same time the legitimacy of the borders established in 1949 on the basis of armistice lines was strongly reinforced. The legitimacy of Israeli rule over the West Bank and Gaza Strip was further undermined from the late 1980s by the Palestinian uprising, the intifada, and a combination of external and internal pressures on both Israel and the Palestinians ultimately paved the way for the start of the Oslo peace process in 1993.

The concept underlying the Oslo peace process was the principle of land for peace – in particular, the idea that Israeli withdrawal from a large part of the territories it occupied in the war of 1967 would pave the way for the creation of Palestinian political institutions. The hope was that this would both free Israel from the burden of occupying areas populated by politically rightless Palestinians and provide an outlet for Palestinian aspirations. Though the final status of the areas taken over by the Palestinians was a matter for negotiation, a widespread assumption was that the agreement was a stepping stone to the creation of a two-state solution to the conflict. The peace process broke down in 2000, when negotiations to arrive at a final settlement ended in failure and recrimination. However, well before the Camp David talks, confidence in the peace process had diminished among both Israeli Jews and Palestinians. Despite the evident breakdown of trust between the parties, the West has been reluctant to accept that the peace process has failed, and efforts continued during the 2000s to revive it. This issue is considered further in Chapter 8.

A fundamental obstacle to the success of the peace process has been the relative political weakness of the Palestinians. That has been reflected in the incapacity of Palestinian negotiators to secure support for the minimal concessions required to give credibility to the two-state solution. But even if Palestinians had been strong enough to secure the return of Israel to its pre-1967 borders, familiar drawbacks of a solution based on partition would remain. In particular, there would remain a considerable Palestinian population within Israel, even if generous incentives were given to Palestinians to move to the newly independent Palestinian state, and even assuming no right of return for Palestinian refugees. As it is, the size of the Israeli Palestinian population has long been a concern of the Israeli right, which has been reflected in proposals for 'transfer' (in this context, a euphemism for expulsion), as well as generating demands that these citizens should be required to acknowledge the Jewish character of the Israeli state.

Also relevant in this context is the argument advanced by Meron Benvenisti in the 1980s that 'the Israeli–Arab conflict, which for forty years has been a region-wide, inter-state conflict, has shrunk to its original core, Israeli–Palestinian intercommunal strife' (Benvenisti 1990: 118). To put it another way, the greater Israel that emerged from the 1967 war had become by the 1980s a deeply divided society and not, as some still saw it, two societies contained within one territory. While Benvenisti did not rule out partition as part of the solution, along with power-sharing, to the inter-communal conflict, a clear implication of his analysis was that the extent of economic interdependence that had developed between Israeli Jews and Palestinians, whether living in the occupied territories or within Israel's pre-1967 boundaries, would make the complete political separation of the two communities impossible to achieve.

The Failure of Apartheid

Apartheid South Africa epitomises the more usual case of international rejection of the legitimacy of partition to address a society's divisions. In the era of decolonisation, which followed the end of the Second World War, South African governments could no longer justify the denial of basic political rights to the country's African, coloured and Indian population by relying on Western sympathy for the doctrine of white racial superiority. The policy of apartheid, which initially had been primarily directed at halting the erosion of segregation, was developed into a programme for preserving white control of the country by changing the framework. The basic idea was to divide Africans – who, when viewed as a racial group, constituted a majority of the country's population – into their ethnic components and then to treat ethnicity as the foundation for the division of the country into new polities. The African reserves were redefined as ethnic homelands that would provide the territorial basis for Africans to exercise their political rights as members of a particular ethnic group. By assigning every African to an ethnic homeland and then granting independence to all the homelands, this grand design held out the prospect of creating a slightly smaller South Africa, since the homelands constituted approximately 13 per cent of the land area of the country, but one in which there would not be a single African citizen, once the process was complete (Giliomee and Schlemmer 1989: 98–9). Since whites outnumbered coloureds and Indians combined, the hope of apartheid's ideologues was that, even without having to address the issue of where coloureds and Indians fitted into the framework, they could create a polity that whites would permanently dominate, while being in outward conformity with the liberal–democratic norms of the West.

In practice, the grand design encountered many problems of implementation. The relatively small area of the country covered by the homelands undermined its credibility as the basis for a just or fair response to the political aspirations of the majority of the population. And the government was never able to persuade the outside world that the country's African population wished to be divided up ethnically for the purpose of the exercise of its political rights. Up to a point, the timing of the start of the implementation of the grand design played a part in its rejection within the West. In the 1960s, ethno-nationalism by no means enjoyed the political credibility it acquired after the end of the Cold War. In Western Europe the advocates of regional nationalism and ethno-nationalism still had not recovered from the discredit resulting from the tactical alliances that had been made by some of their number with the Nazis during the Second World War. In Eastern Europe the communist system kept a lid on expressions of rival political ideologies, including ethno-nationalism. In the United States the 1960s was the era of the civil rights movement, which advocated integration and an end to segregation. That ran counter to the emphasis of ethno-nationalism on political separation and on the preservation of the specific cultural identity of the ethnic group.

However, the more important factor in the rejection of nationalism was its obvious lack of legitimacy within South Africa itself. The government's commitment to ethnic partition did not generate support among the African population for credible ethno-nationalist movements. Thus the government was hard put even to find leaders within the homelands ready to operate the structures it created in furtherance of its grand design, which smacked too obviously of a divide-and-rule policy. Ironically, the one ethnically based political grouping with a strong popular following, the Zulu Inkatha movement, had been adamant in opposing homeland independence. The large element of self-interest in the government's interpretation of ethnicity was evident from the outset. Through the slippery use of the notion of population groups, it emphasised ethnic divisions among Africans, while glossing over their existence among whites. In an attempt to impress world opinion in the aftermath of the damage done to its reputation by the

Sharpeville massacre, the government moved rapidly to grant self-government to the Transkei as the ethnic homeland of the Xhosas in 1963. One consequence of this was the exclusion of Xhosa-speaking reserves to the west of the Kei River. They ultimately formed the basis of a second Xhosa homeland, Ciskei. Another consequence was that the Transkei encompassed a significant South Sotho minority. And in fact none of the homelands established by the government ever became entirely ethnically homogeneous, despite enforced movement of population on a large scale.

During the South African transition between 1990 and 1994, a significant ethnically based party emerged to challenge the African National Congress (ANC). This was the Inkatha Freedom Party (IFP), which developed out of the Zulu Inkatha movement. The party won over 10 per cent of the national vote in the elections of 1994 and was the largest party in the province of KwaZulu Natal in terms of its share of the vote. For a period, it seemed possible that the party might use its support in the province to further an ethno-nationalist agenda that might include seeking secession from South Africa. However, at subsequent elections support for the IFP fell back, and with it any possibility that the party might present a challenge to South Africa's territorial integrity. Yet the possibility remains that, if support for the ANC declines at future elections, the regional concentration of the country's minorities, as well as the vertical divisions among ethnic groups within the African majority, might encourage opposition parties to adopt separatist agendas.

Boost to Separatism

The significance of the West's shift in attitude towards secession can hardly be overstated in this context. The anathema against secession that the West maintained during the years of the Cold War has fallen by the wayside. This has given a huge boost to separatist movements. It presents governments in deeply divided societies, as well as in simply plural societies, with a profound dilemma, particularly in cases of vertical divisions with a territorial dimension. If governments seek to accommodate minorities though the grant of autonomy to a particular region or the like, they run the risk that this step will facilitate and give credibility to quests for secession. In particular, should a nationalist movement succeed in securing majority support within the boundaries of an autonomous region for independence, the movement will have established a strong claim for the independence of the territory in question on the basis of the precedents that have been set since 1990. Admittedly, demonstrating such support may be problematic. Thus India has resisted the holding of a plebiscite on the status of Kashmir since it was first proposed as a way of resolving the dispute over the region.

A further recourse for states faced by the growth of nationalist sentiment among minorities in peripheral regions is to encourage settlement by members of the majority population in these regions to counter the threat of separatism. This approach has been taken by China, with large settlements of Han Chinese in both Tibet and Xinjiang. An outcome of the process has been a high level of antagonism towards the settlers, as incomers put there to secure the regions for the centre. What is emerging in each of the autonomous regions within the constraints of China's authoritarian political system is a deeply divided society.

Another way in which states can anticipate the growth of separatist sentiment among minorities is to ensure that the boundaries of units to which power is devolved from the centre are drawn so as to minimise that possibility. Ensuring that the boundaries do not coincide with ethnic divisions is one way of doing this. It may also provide another route to the creation of a deeply divided society at a regional level. While it may be objected that state stratagems that prevent freely constituted and self-defined communities from exercising their right to self-determination are illegitimate, power politics and geo-strategic considerations remain a basic obstacle to the constant redrawing of boundaries in accordance with changes of popular sentiment. In any case, boundary change is more commonly a factor in the creation of deeply divided societies than a way of resolving their problems.

7 POWER-SHARING AND POLITICAL ACCOMMODATION

As was discussed in the Introduction, widespread use of the concept 'deeply divided societies' was connected with the thesis that special mechanisms were needed if democracy was to flourish in such societies. The most far-reaching of these special mechanisms that have been proposed in this context is the consociational model, as primarily developed by Arend Lijphart. His model was initially propounded to explain the stability of a number of small European democracies. In other words, it was developed in the first instance to enrich typologies of the different forms of liberal democracy following on from the work of Gabriel Almond. The arrangements adopted differed in detail from country to country, but the resemblances among them provided Lijphart with the building blocks for his model. Of course, the political elites in these countries had arrived at their respective answers to the problem of democratic governance in a segmented society without the benefit of Lijphart's model or his theoretical justification of it. This is not to belittle Lijphart's achievement, but rather to draw attention to the fact that a number of the practices associated with consociationalism flow quite naturally from the dilemmas that face many societies going through a process of democratisation, particularly if these societies are also marked by deep divisions of one kind or another.

The growth of the influence of consociationalism stemmed from another consideration: the failure of the Westminster model of democracy in many newly independent countries. Though there were a wide variety of reasons for the breakdown of democracy in these developing countries, the majoritarian nature of the Westminster model was recognised as a contributing factor in a number of cases. In particular, the effective working of majoritarian systems depended on the prospect that parties could be voted in and out of office – in short, that, periodically, there was alternation between the parties in power. This presented an obvious difficulty in a society in which voting followed the lines of an ethnic or other segmental division, since in such a society the outcome of elections was to a degree predetermined. In such places there were likely to be both permanent majorities and, more importantly, permanent minorities, without any prospect of participation in government. Elected governments had little reason to pay attention to minority interests and every reason to focus on those of the majority group, since the most serious political challenge such a government was likely to face was from within the majority group, if it was not sufficiently assiduous in favouring the interests of the majority. A case in point is political competition among Sinhala-based political parties in post-independence Sri Lanka. The end result of government that consistently gave precedence to the interests of the Sinhala majority was a revolt by members of the Tamil minority as elements of the minority sought to exit the political system.

Consociationalism

In circumstances in which the outcome of elections repeatedly resembles an ethnic census, the danger is considerable that groups excluded from power will be alienated from the political system and the legitimacy of the system will be undermined. There are various ways in which this problem can be addressed in the design of political institutions. As indicated above, the consociational model is one of the most elaborate. It will be considered first. In a work elaborating on his initial formulation of the model, Lijphart detailed the four elements of consociational democracy as follows:

> The first and most important element is government by a grand coalition of the political leaders of all significant segments of the plural society. This can take several different forms, such as a grand coalition cabinet in a parliamentary system, a "grand" council or committee with important advisory functions, or a grand coalition of a president and other top officeholders in a presidential system. The other three basic elements of consociational democracy are (1) the mutual veto or "concurrent majority" rule, which serves as an additional protection of vital minority interests, (2) proportionality as the principal standard of political representation, civil service appointment, and allocation of public funds, and (3) a high degree of autonomy for each segment to run its own internal affairs. (Lijphart 1977, 25)

In explaining how such systems had come into existence in a number of countries during the process of democratisation, Lijphart identified a number of favourable conditions for the emergence and functioning of consociational democracy.

> On the basis of a comparative examination of the four European cases of consociational and other Western democracies, the following factors appear to be particularly important in this respect: a multiple balance of power, small size of the country involved, overarching loyalties, segmental isolation, prior traditions of elite accommodation, and – although much more weakly and ambiguously – the presence of crosscutting cleavages. To the extent that these factors contribute to cooperation among segmental leaders and loyal support by the followers in the segments, they are conditions that are helpful not only in establishing consociational democracy in a plural society but also, once it is established, in maintaining and strengthening it. (Lijphart 1977, 54)

In his writings, Lijphart combines historical analysis of the circumstances that led to the emergence of consociational democracy in a number of small European countries with advocacy of consociationalism as a means of conflict resolution. Thus he has taken great pains to argue that even the absence of all the favourable conditions he has identified is not an insuperable barrier to the adoption of a consociational democracy as a successful vehicle for resolving conflict. This reflects the importance he attaches to the exercise of political will in determining whether a consociational solution is possible. Even though he accepts that, in the most difficult cases of deeply divided societies, any kind of democracy may be difficult to achieve, he contends that precisely in such cases consociationalism offers the best, if not the only, prospect of a democratic outcome. However, at the same time, in instances when consociational democracy has broken down when adopted as an instrument of conflict resolution, Lijphart has been ready to explain its failure by recourse to the favourable conditions for its operation – which he identified on the basis of his original cases.

For example, following the collapse of the power-sharing executive in Northern Ireland in May 1974, Lijphart pondered over the reasons for this failure in a long review article on Northern Ireland in the *British Journal of Political Science*. He argued that three factors conducive to consociational democracy were altogether lacking in Northern Ireland. They were '(1) a multiple balance of power [. . .] (2) acceptability of the grand-coalition form of government [. . .] and (3) some degree of national solidarity' (Lijphart 1975, 99–100). And he contended, further, that, while it appeared that three factors conducive to consociational democracy were present in Northern Ireland, on further examination they did not provide support for the success of consociationalism. These factors were '(1) a small population [. . .] (2) distinct lines of cleavage [. . .] and (3) external threats to the country' (pp. 100–1).

In relation to the first set of factors, there was, self-evidently, little basis for a multiple balance of power in Northern Ireland as a society divided between a dominant majority community and a minority subordinate community, while as of 1975 it was also plainly the case that most Protestants opposed the notion that the minority should be guaranteed representation in the government of Northern Ireland. This outlook Lijphart attributed in part to their attachment to the British political model with its emphasis on majoritarianism. Finally, the conflicting communities in Northern Ireland were divided in their national identities. In relation to the second set of factors, Lijphart suggested firstly that Northern Ireland was too small to generate the political talent required for the operation of consociational democracy. He contended secondly that the intensity of political competition within each of the cleavages prevented the elites from developing the freedom of manoeuvre they needed to do a deal across the province's sectarian divide.

More convincingly Lijphart argued that the external threat to the existence of Northern Ireland was not conducive to cooperation.

> The proposition that foreign threats may produce an impetus toward consociationalism is based on the idea that such threats may impress on quarrelling elites the need for unity and co-operation. The Northern Ireland regime has been under the continuous external threat – albeit not a very grave one – of the Republic's constitutional claim to the province. But this has not produced co-operative attitudes. The obvious modification which the proposition needs is that an external threat must be perceived as a common danger by all of the subcultures in order to have a unifying effect. Otherwise, as in the case of Northern Ireland, it will only serve to widen the differences between subcultures. (Lijphart 1975, 101)

Lijphart concluded his review by proposing the partition of Northern Ireland as the only durable solution to the problem, given that he saw integration as a pipe dream in such a severely divided society and that he had demonstrated the difficulties in the way of a consociational outcome.

As it turned out, for once in his life, Lijphart was overly pessimistic about the prospects for consociationalism. The British government learnt lessons from the failure of the Sunningdale Agreement of December 1973, and in co-operation with the Irish government it tried again to establish a consociational system of government in Northern Ireland following ceasefires by the main republican and loyalist paramilitary organisations in 1994. The result was the Belfast Agreement of April 1998. As discussed in the previous chapter, implementation of the deal, which one of the participants in the negotiations wittily described as 'Sunningdale for slow learners', encountered numerous difficulties and the system only became secure after the final crisis over the devolution of policing and justice powers was overcome in 2010. However, despite the suspension of its consociational institutions and the imposition of direct rule from London for long periods since 1998, the Belfast Agreement has come to be seen as a model for the resolution of conflict.

As well as the lengthy suspensions, critics of the Belfast Agreement can point to the process of political polarisation that has occurred under the implementation of the deal. This is evident in the four elections to the Northern Ireland Assembly that have occurred since 1998. The Assembly provides the foundation of devolved government in Northern Ireland, with the executive elected from its members employing the d'Hondt formula for determining the representation of the parties and their choice of ministerial portfolios. The formula effectively ensures representation in the executive of the main parties in the Assembly. The Assembly itself is elected from Northern Ireland's 18 Westminster constituencies: six members are elected from each constituency. The electoral system is the single transferable vote system of proportional representation, a system helpful to minor parties by comparison either with the 'first past the post' system or with the alternative vote. That makes the polarisation that has occurred since 1998 all the more striking. At the time of the Belfast Agreement the Ulster Unionist Party and the Social Democratic and Labour Party were the dominant parties on their respective sides of the sectarian divide. They were overtaken in 2003 by their more radical counterparts, the Democratic Unionist Party and Sinn Féin. The hold of the two radical parties grew even stronger in 2007 and 2011, as Table 7.1 underlines. At the same time the stance of the two radical parties has become more accommodating to the functioning of the Belfast Agreement, albeit it has been amended in a number of ways so as to address their views and interests. In the elections of 2011 both radical parties stressed the role they had played in making devolved government work.

External Conflict Management

In a book on the role that consociationalism has played in the Northern Ireland peace process, with a particular focus on the work of its most prominent academic proponents, Brendan O'Leary and John McGarry, Rupert Taylor notes, from the internet search he conducted, that Northern Ireland was the most widely cited example of consociationalism in

Table 7.1   Results of elections to Northern Ireland Assembly under the
Belfast Agreement, indicating seats won by main parties and showing
polarisation of opinion

Party/Year	1998	2003	2007	2011
Democratic Unionist Party	20	30	36	38
Sinn Féin	18	24	26	29
Ulster Unionist Party	28	27	18	16
Social Democratic and Labour Party	24	18	16	14
Alliance Party	6	6	7	8
Others	12	3	3	3
TOTAL	108	108	108	108

SOURCE Information taken from Nicholas Whyte, 'Elections Northern Ireland',
available at http://www.ark.ac.uk/elections/

scholarly publications (Taylor 2009: 8). As he also underlines, Northern
Ireland was part of a new wave of consociationalism following the end
of the Cold War. Other current cases identified by Taylor are Bosnia-
Herzegovina (1995–), Burundi (1998–), Macedonia (2000–), Afghanistan
(2004–), Iraq (2005–) and Kenya (2008–) (p. 6). The list provides an indication of the loose usage of consociationalism: it may be employed to
describe practically any situation in which there is power-sharing among
the major political factions in a society, regardless of whether this is
entrenched on a permanent basis in a constitutional document or is simply
a temporary political expedient. What these cases also have in common is
the role that external parties have played in bringing about power-sharing,
sometimes in the face of considerable internal resistance. The role of
external mediation is explored more fully in the next chapter, but the irony
of this development is worth underlining here.

A powerful motivation for the adoption of consociationalism in Lijphart's
original cases was as a means of preserving the independence and survival
of small states. In other words, consociationalism was generated internally
by political elites that recognised the dangers of unrestrained political
competition in a democratic setting, given the polity's social divisions. The
use of consociational devices was facilitated by the prior existence of a
tradition of political accommodation among the elites or, in the case of
Austria, by political elites' recognition of the disastrous consequences of
their failure to act with restraint in a previous period. By contrast, in the
new wave the initiative for the employment of consociational devices has
come from outside the society. And instead of consociationalism being the

product of political accommodation, the objective of its external sponsors is that the operation of consociational devices will facilitate the growth of political accommodation among the political elites and more widely. Further, far from being a means of preserving the country's independence, consociationalism can be seen in the cases of the new wave as an instrument of external conflict management.

Northern Ireland is a special case in this context, since Northern Ireland is not, and has never been, an independent state. Further, the option of independence enjoys little support in either of the province's two communities. Yet Northern Ireland clearly remains a place apart from the rest of the United Kingdom, and it is reasonable to describe the role of the British and Irish governments working together as external conflict managers. In Taylor's other cases in the new wave, apart from Kenya, the presence of external military forces was germane to the adoption of consociational devices, and it is questionable whether such devices would have been adopted in any of these cases in the absence of external pressure. And, even though there was no international military presence to influence parties in the case of Kenya, external pressure played a part in this case as well.

The Kenyan government was pressed to accept power-sharing in the wake of a disputed presidential election in December 2007. The incumbent, Mwai Kibaki, was officially declared to have been re-elected. However, his principal opponent, Raila Odinga, claimed that he had won. The results of a number of opinion polls as well as of an exit poll lent credibility to his charge that extensive rigging of the outcome had occurred during the count that had robbed him of victory. Extensive violence followed the elections. Hundreds of people died in the violence, which had an ethnic dimension that reflected the ethnic differences in the support bases of the two candidates. This aspect of the violence aggravated fears that the violence might spiral out of control in the absence of a political resolution over the outcome. In the wake of external mediation by the former Secretary-General of the United Nations Kofi Annan, Odinga was prevailed upon to accept the position of prime minister within a power-sharing government in which Kibaki remained president.

A somewhat similar outcome occurred in Zimbabwe after disputed elections. Following South African mediation, the government and the opposition agreed to a power-sharing deal in September 2008. But, whereas both the American and the British governments were well disposed towards power-sharing in Kenya and had a generally favourable view of Kibaki's leadership in Kenya, they disliked the arrangements in Zimbabwe as permitting Robert Mugabe to retain a hold on power. In two other cases of disputed election results in the 2000s, the West sought a reversal of the outcome that had been officially proclaimed. The first of these was Ukraine. Widespread protests followed the official declaration of Ukraine's November 2004 Presidential election. This maintained that the government-backed candidate, Viktor Yanukovych, had defeated the challenger, Viktor Yushchenko. The Orange Revolution, as it was dubbed, was successful in forcing a re-run of the election, which was won by Yushchenko. But divisions in the coalition supporting Yushchenko paved the way for a comeback by Yanukovych, who was elected president in February 2010. The second was the case of Ivory Coast. In the country's long delayed presidential election of November 2010, the opposition leader, Alassane Ouattarra, was proclaimed the winner of the poll by the country's electoral commission. However, this outcome was reversed by the Constitutional Council, which disqualified a large number of the votes that had been cast for Ouattara in the north of the country and reinstated the incumbent, Laurent Gbagbo. Most of the outside world supported the claims of Ouattara to have won the contest and rejected Gbagbo's insistence that there should be negotiations for a power-sharing government along the lines of the deal agreed in Kenya in 2008. In this case, the views of the outside world prevailed. French military support for Ouattara helped to ensure that the forces supporting Gbagbo were defeated militarily and the denouement was that Laurent Gbagbo was taken into custody (Smith 2011).

It is possible to argue in each of these cases that the polarisation of opinion that was evident in the elections reflected a deep social divide. There were ethnic and territorial dimensions to this divide in each case. The core of Kibaki's supporters comprised Kikuyu in the centre of Kenya, while Odinga's political base lay among the Luo in the west of the country. In Zimbabwe, opposition to Mugabe was especially strong in the urban areas and among the Matabele in the West of the country. In Ukraine, too, there was an east–west divide, with supporters of the Orange Revolution in the west, while Yanukovych has drawn his support from the east of the country and among Russian speakers. In Ivory Coast the divide was between a Christian south and a Muslim north. Ivory Coast had a long record of stability after independence under the leadership of Félix Houphouët-Boigny, but after his death the country had succumbed to civil war in the 2000s, which had prompted international intervention. Ivory Coast was the latest of these countries to experience substantial levels of political violence. Each of the other cases had experienced high levels of violence in earlier phases of their history. However, for the most part this violence was unrelated to their present divisions, while the absence of a separatist agenda among the contenders for power provides a further reason for questioning whether they should be included in the category of deeply divided societies.

But, in any event, this question has not been a major consideration in international responses to crises in these societies, or in the devising of institutional arrangements to meet the needs of the society in question. Rather, geo-strategic calculations have been at the fore in determining the attitudes of the Western powers and in shaping their interventions. To be fair, a prime concern has simply been to end violent conflict, in view of its wider destabilising potential and its spill-over effects in terms of refugees. This has also meant that priority has been given to addressing the immediate situation, in which the existing balance of political forces loomed large, and the history of the society has consequently tended to be disregarded. Thus, in the case of deeply divided Kosovo, the claims of the Serb minority (and the process by which their numbers had been reduced over a long period) received little recognition, while in Bosnia-Herzegovina elaborate consociational arrangements were established in a society where, prior to the conflict of the early 1990s, there had been extensive integration among Bosniacs, Serbs and Croats that was reflected in inter-marriage among members of the three communities.

Admittedly, the conflict itself, which arose out of the breakup of Yugoslavia, had a drastic impact on relations among the communities. This has been succinctly described by Rob Aitken.

In Bosnia-Herzogovina ethno-nationalist propaganda about the oppression of Christians under Muslims and Second World War atrocities emphasized the boundaries between 'Serbs', 'Croats' and 'Muslims', and placed the blame for perceived past wrongs on contemporary ethnic 'others'. Furthermore, the targeting of mosques and cultural buildings during the war destroyed not only physical evidence of Muslim presence in particular localities, but also of centuries of shared culture and social life. The targeting of cultural buildings sought to rewrite history and deny that the different ethnic categories had ever lived together peacefully. Not only were boundaries between ethnic categories sharpened during the Bosnian war, the social and religious category of 'Muslim' was transformed into a Bosniac national identity. In the process religious background, cultural identity and political loyalties were conflated, (Aitken 2010: 236)

Entrenching Divisions

The argument put forward by Aitken is that in this and other cases the imposition of consociational settlements has tended to entrench the ethnic divisions that arose in the course of the conflict. In an article comparing the cases of Bosnia-Herzegovina, Afghanistan and Iraq, Aitken summarises the nub of his thesis as follows:

Assumptions about ethnicity made by international policy-makers have a significant impact on post-conflict situations. International policy-makers have in the past accepted the image of ethnicity as a relatively fixed political identity. Rather than focusing on the ways in which conflicts have ethnicized people and raised the salience of ethnicity, they have accepted[,] or even imposed, an ethnic framing of the conflict. In the process it is implicitly assumed that the patterns of ethnic divisions at the end of the conflict are permanent. This then defines post-conflict societies as ethnically divided societies and representative government as being the representation of ethnic groups. In this context peace-building in attempting to produce legitimate representative government has institutionalized ethnic politics. (Aitken 2007, 262)

Three points may be made in response to Aitken's argument. Firstly, the arrangements for the governance of these societies that were devised in the aftermath of conflict were strongly influenced by the political realities that confronted the outside powers on the ground. The role of consociational theory and that of assumptions about the nature of the society appear to have been secondary. At the same time, the outside powers did recognise the advantages of a broadly consociational approach from the perspective of external conflict management. Secondly, it can be argued that after its war Bosnia-Herzegovina had become a deeply divided society, whatever the case may have been beforehand, and that the new realities provided a justification for special mechanisms to dampen down inter-communal conflict. The picture in this respect is less clear-cut in the case of Iraq and Afghanistan, given the history of divisions in these societies. Thirdly, proponents of consociationalism might contend that the institutionalisation of ethnic politics is not intended to be permanent and that in the long run the achievement of political accommodation under consociationalism will make it possible to do without its mechanisms, as the examples of the Netherlands and Austria have shown.

However, cases in which consociationalism has ended because of its success are few and far between. Further, it is open to argument that the cases where this has happened were not deeply divided societies, so prompting the charge that consociationalism has only succeeded where it was not really needed. Cases of the breakdown of consociationalism in deeply divided societies include Cyprus in 1963, Northern Ireland in 1974 and Lebanon in 1975. However, these failures need to be seen in the context of the difficulty of establishing stable government in such societies, let alone legitimate constitutional governments. They also need to be seen in the wider context of the breakdown of democracies. As underlined in the 2000s by the cases of Iraq and Afghanistan, the staging of competitive multi-party elections is only a first step in the establishment of a democracy. The consolidation of democracy into a widely accepted and legitimate form of government is a much larger challenge. The presence of foreign forces may appear to be essential to the holding of free and fair elections, but at the same time their presence may also make it impossible for the members of a government that emerges from such elections to establish their credibility as authentic representatives of a population under occupation and thus to be capable of advancing the legitimacy of the political system.

A more general problem, which explains why the breakdown of democracy is such a widespread phenomenon, is the frequent reluctance of democratically elected governments to permit their removal from office through the ballot box. Alternation in power is an important test for any majoritarian system, and many democracies have foundered over it. The violent conflicts that result from governments' clinging to power often do have an ethnic or communal dimension. One consequence may be the creation of a deeply divided society as a result of the experience of widespread inter-communal violence and the legacy it leaves. However, to attribute the breakdown of democracy to ethnic or communal antagonism may be to confuse cause and effect. In short, ethnic mobilisation may be the last resort of government or opposition in circumstances where the legitimacy of the system has already been brought into question. Why governments should be less willing to give up power voluntarily in some societies rather than others is, of course, an important question in this context. One explanation is that government offers one of the few ways to access wealth in a poor society, thereby increasing what is at stake for itself and for its close associates in the loss of power. It is worth stressing that this problem exists quite independently of whether the society is homogeneous or not, though its consequences may be affected by how divided the society is.

Territorial Approaches

Consociationalism is by no means the only approach that may be taken to address ethnic or other communal differences in a polity. Thus, particularly in societies with vertical divisions, a territorial approach may be taken through the establishment of a multi-level system of governance in which power is divided between the centre and the regions. Admittedly, consociationalism often includes a territorial dimension under the principle of segmental autonomy. For example, Bosnia-Herzegovina is a consociational federation. However, not all consociational systems are federal, and many federations are not consociational in their design. In fact, most full-scale federations do not lend themselves to consociationalism. In particular, they tend to be large in population and in size, whereas a feature of the cases on which Lijphart based the concept of consociationalism was that they were small European countries compared to larger and more powerful neighbours. However, the accommodation of minorities in territorial terms can take many forms that fall short of full-scale federation, including the creation of autonomous regions for particular minorities.

The boundaries of the units of a federation may not coincide with ethnic or other communal divisions in a society. It may simply not be feasible to create such units because of the dispersed territorial distribution of different communities across the society – or because the boundaries may be largely pre-determined, as in the case of existing polities joining together to form a federation. Ethnic or communal criteria may just be absent from the criteria employed in the drawing of the boundaries between units. Alternatively, it may be deliberate policy on the part of the state not to concentrate minorities within single units that might provide a platform for the minority to make demands on the centre or to seek to exit the state. But some states are what John Coakley terms 'ethnic federations' (Coakley 2010: 194). Most states in the world are not federations in the first place. Coakley suggests that the current number of federations is 24, though this includes what he acknowledges to be the borderline cases of Spain and South Africa. The expansion of the powers of the regions in Spain since the country's transition to democracy provides greater justification for its inclusion than that of South Africa. In post-apartheid South Africa, the political impetus for additional decentralisation of power to the provinces remains weak.

Among these, Coakley singled out 10 cases in which one or more of the units played a role in the accommodation of ethnic or cultural differences. His list included the two consociational federations, Bosnia-Herzegovina and Belgium. The other cases identified by Coakley were the Russian Federation, Switzerland, Spain, Canada, Ethiopia, Nigeria, India and Pakistan. Of all of these cases, Switzerland appears by far the most stable – in terms of agreement on the shape of the system, the functioning of government on a day-to-day basis and the boundaries of the country itself. The remaining cases can be described, to varying degrees, as work in progress. And their survival in the long term remains an open question, not least because of their relatively recent history. The Russian Federation emerged out of the breakup of the Soviet Union in the 1990s and remains threatened by a number of secessionist movements, particularly in the Caucasus. Bosnia-Herzegovina came into existence when Yugoslavia, another case of ethnic federation, broke up in the same decade. Coakley succinctly describes the fragile nature of Bosnia-Herzegovina as a polity as follows:

> Bosnia-Herzegovina, a loose federation of two entities (an ethnic Muslim–Croat federation and a 'Serbian Republic') has been sustained since the Dayton Agreement of 1995 more by international pressure than by the will of its peoples to live together. (Coakley 2010: 202)

India and Pakistan became independent states with the partition of colonial India in 1947, while Pakistan suffered further partition in the 1970s, with the secession of Bangladesh. The violent conflict in Kashmir is both a challenge to the territorial integrity of India and a source of tension with Pakistan. Pakistan also has separatist movements seeking an exit from the polity. After a change in regime in the aftermath of the Cold War, the boundaries of Ethiopia also changed, in the 1990s, with the agreed exit of Eritrea. In the same decade, the survival of Canada hung by a thread: there was a very narrow defeat of a referendum on Quebec's quest for sovereignty in 1995. Nigeria was afflicted by civil war over the attempted secession of Biafra in the 1960s. The legacy of the conflict still casts a shadow over the survival of the country within its current boundaries.

Belgium was one of the four European countries on which Lijphart based the concept of consociationalism. However, whereas the success of consociationalism enabled the neighbouring state of the Netherlands to overcome its divisions to the point where reliance on power-sharing was no longer needed to maintain political stability, the operation of consociationalism in Belgium has become increasingly fraught. That has been reflected in increasing political polarisation between Flemings and Walloons, which has led to difficulty in agreeing to the formation of governments. It should be noted that the ethno-linguistic division at the heart of political conflict in Belgium today is different from the class and religious differences that provided the original basis for Belgium's consociational institutions. But, despite the intensity of this relatively new conflict, it has not as yet manifested itself in the lethal political violence that would mark Belgium out as a deeply divided society.

Though the final terms of the powers of the regions are by no means settled in the case of Spain, this country stands out as the most successful of these cases in achieving political accommodation through the establishment of autonomous regions in Catalonia, Galicia and the Basque Country. Political violence in support of a nationalist quest for the creation of a Basque homeland preceded Spain's transition to democracy, and there was an escalation in the level of violence after Franco's death and in the early years of Spanish democracy. While the campaign of violence for independence largely petered out in the late 2000s, with only episodic acts of lethal violence attributable to the Basque conflict, the problem of the relatively weak Basque attachment to the Spanish state remains. Luis Moreno has argued that a key to the success of this form of accommodation has been the existence of dual identity. For example, he has shown that only a relatively small minority of people in Catalonia consider themselves exclusively Catalan or Spanish in terms of their identity. And he has applied what has been dubbed 'the Moreno question' to other cases. In particular, he has demonstrated that dual identity underpins the operation of devolved government in Scotland, with a majority of Scots considering themselves to be both Scottish and British, whether equally or predominantly one or the other (Moreno 2006). The United Kingdom provides an example of a previously unitary state devolving power territorially in late 1990s to accommodate Scottish and Welsh identities in response to the growth of nationalism, but without the adoption of a fully fledged federal system of government.

Accommodating Linguistic and Religious Differences

The territorial approach to the accommodation of social cleavages is most likely to be feasible in cases where an ethnic or otherwise culturally distinct minority is concentrated in a particular region. Vertical divisions involving language provide the commonest examples. The existence of regional government provides a ready-made forum in which minority languages may be accorded recognition. Attitudes towards linguistic diversity have undergone substantial change in the course of the last 40 years. The imposition of one language on a society in the name of nation-building is no longer considered an acceptable approach by states to language diversity within a country's borders. The adoption in 1992, under the auspices of the Council of Europe, of the European Charter for Regional or Minority Languages is an indication of the change that has taken place towards the status of local languages. Whereas the survival of Europe's lesser known languages had previously been seen as an obstacle to national cohesion in the states in which they were spoken, their preservation is now viewed in a positive light, as enriching society's cultural heritage.

However, it should be noted that the Charter does not apply to the languages spoken by immigrants. Thus it is not an obstacle to states promoting the absorption of immigrants through the encouragement of proficiency in the dominant language. Nor does it apply to the protection of minority languages that have already been adopted as an official language of the state at the national level, as in the example of Irish in the Republic of Ireland. As in the case of multiculturalism more generally, the change in attitudes towards the promotion of language diversity has not gone uncontested. It has provoked a backlash in a number of countries. For example, in a number of states in the United States of America, resolutions have been adopted that English should be made the country's sole official language, partly in response to the growth of use of Spanish in states with large Hispanic minorities. In a speech to the Munich Security Conference in February 2011, British Prime Minister David Cameron criticised the toleration of segregated communities as a consequence of 'the doctrine of state multiculturalism' (Cameron 2011). He also emphasised the importance of immigrants learning English.

But providing immigrants with information in their own languages to help their initial absorption in the society is not incompatible with encouraging them to learn the dominant language in a state. And, in any event, the incentives for immigrants to understand the dominant language of the host society remain very strong. English enjoys the further advantage of being the dominant lingua franca in the world. This has led to the adoption of English as an official language in countries in which it had previously been the mother tongue of a tiny minority of the population. Two examples are Namibia and Rwanda. English occupies a privileged position in the realm of languages with the waning of the influence of the notion that a limited number of languages should be regarded as representative of high culture while the rest tend to be dismissed as unsuitable for modern communication (Safran 2010: 25).

Another common source of vertical divisions is religion. Adherents of the major branches of the world's main religions tend to be quite widely dispersed, but those of more minor faiths or branches may be associated with particular regions of a country. In such cases, the territorial approach may provide a convenient means of accommodating such minorities. A notable example of changes to a country's internal boundaries was the decision of India to divide Punjab in 1966. The effect was to create an entity in which Sikhs constitute a majority, though it should be acknowledged that the rationale for this change was language as much as religion. But in any event this territorial adjustment made by the Indian central government in response to demands from below was not immediately successful in conciliating Sikhs who had become alienated from India. Indeed, violent conflict with Sikh separatists followed that culminated in the storming of the Golden Temple in Amritsar by the Indian army and in the subsequent assassination of Indian Prime Minister Indira Gandhi, in revenge, in 1984.

An issue much debated is whether the territorial approach constitutes an effective means of political accommodation or simply whets the appetite of separatists for further concessions. The latter proposition was central to opposition to the establishment of devolved governments in Scotland and Wales, but with the functioning of devolved government this argument has lost much of its force, despite the formation of a Scottish National Party government in Scotland after the elections of 2007. But this is a topic on which it is difficult to arrive at definitive conclusions, since it is hard to disentangle the impact of institutional design on political developments from other factors. Somewhat similarly, John Coakley concludes his survey of whether ethnic federations promote or impede political stability by stating that the evidence on their effects is mixed and that no broad comparative conclusion can be drawn (Coakley 2010: 206–7). But it is apparent from this discussion that the territorial approach, by itself, is no more a panacea for the problems of deeply divided societies than is consociationalism in its various elements.

A limitation of the territorial approach is that the regions created for the purposes of accommodating particular groups are rarely homogeneous entities. New minorities are inevitably created in the process. Further, in any event, the population of regions, as much as that of countries, is not static. Their demography is subject to change as a result of immigration and emigration, as well as of such factors as differential birth rates among groups. The setting up of a regional government may even facilitate the emergence of a deeply divided society in the territory in question. Northern Ireland might be regarded as a case in point. The creation of a devolved government in Northern Ireland when Ireland was partitioned under the 1920 Government of Ireland Act sharpened sectarian divisions in the province, since the safest way for the Unionist Party to ensure majority support for its rule was to give priority to Protestant unity and therefore to make no concessions to Catholics that might divide Protestant opinion.

However, while it is reasonable to argue that the operation of devolution under a majoritarian system exacerbated the sectarian divide in Northern Ireland, it did not create the division. The divide long predated partition. During Northern Ireland's troubles a significant strand of opinion among unionists favoured integration as a constitutional solution to the conflict. They argued that, if Northern Ireland was treated like any other part of the United Kingdom and the national political parties competed for votes in the province as they did in every other part of the country, the influence of sectarianism on the province's politics would be diminished. In this context, they also argued that it had been a mistake ever to set up a devolved government in Northern Ireland and that Northern Ireland should have been fully integrated constitutionally and politically into the United

Kingdom at the time of partition rather than being treated as a place apart. A weakness in the argument was its assumption that Catholic support for Irish nationalism would have substantially diminished in these circumstances. The argument also underestimated the interest of British political parties in the removal of the Irish question from the country's domestic politics. The possibility of integration was superseded in the 1990s by two developments: the Northern Ireland peace process and Scottish and Welsh devolution.

Another example of a deeply divided society at the level of a regional government is the Indian state of Jammu and Kashmir. It is the only state in India with a Muslim majority. The Indian state comprises the larger part of the princely state partitioned between India and Pakistan shortly after the two countries' independence. Since Jammu and Kashmir's accession to India in the aftermath of the subcontinent's decolonisation, India has resisted demands that a referendum should be held to determine the status of the territory. Approximately two-thirds of the population of the state are Muslims, while nearly 30 per cent are Hindu. There are also small Sikh and Buddhist minorities. The state itself is made up of three distinct regions, the Kashmir Valley, Jammu, and Ladakh. Over half of the population of the state resides in the Kashmir Valley, which was overwhelmingly Muslim even before the expulsion of Kashmir Pandits from the region in the 1990s. The majority in Jammu is Hindu, while Ladakh, which has only a small proportion of the state's population but covers a large area, is divided between Muslims and Buddhists.

In the first 40 years after India's independence, the central government was able to maintain control over the state of Jammu and Kashmir through the pursuit of a divide-and-rule strategy. This was despite simmering resentment at the failure of India to grant the region autonomy and despite the conflict that failure caused with the state's leading political figures, including the Lion of Kashmir, Sheikh Mohammed Abdullah. Until the late 1980s, the Kashmir dispute was largely conceived of as part of the wider international conflict, in the sub-continent, between India and Pakistan. The turning point came with the state legislative elections of 1987. The disputed nature of the elections, with accusations of rigging levelled against the central government, was the catalyst for the launch of an insurgency in the state against Indian rule. But the scale of the internal crisis that followed within the state was unexpected, as Victoria Schofield explained:

The armed insurgency which gathered momentum after the 1987 elections caught the rest of the world unawares. To most onlookers, Kashmir was a tourist spot, a place for rest and relaxation after a hot and exhausting trip through the hotter plains of India. Despite the political discontent at the outcome of the election, in 1987 it remained ostensibly calm. (Schofield 2000: 138)

However, in subsequent years, there was a rapid escalation in the level of violence. As is common in many conflicts, there remain wide differences in the estimates of the numbers that have been killed in the violence and in how they should be categorised. But the figures in Table 7.2 do

Table 7.2   Fatalities in the conflict in Jammu and Kashmir, 1988–2010

Year/Breakdown	Civilians	Security Force Personnel	Terrorists	Total
1988	29	1	1	31
1989	79	13	0	92
1990	862	132	183	1177
1991	594	185	614	1393
1992	859	177	873	1909
1993	1023	216	1328	2567
1994	1012	236	1651	2899
1995	1161	297	1338	2796
1996	1333	376	1194	2903
1997	840	355	1177	2372
1998	877	339	1045	2261
1999	799	555	1184	2538
2000	842	638	1808	3288
2001	1067	590	2850	4507
2002	839	469	1714	3022
2003	658	338	1546	2542
2004	534	325	951	1810
2005	521	218	1000	1739
2006	349	168	599	1116
2007	164	121	492	777
2008	69	90	382	541
2009	55	78	242	375
2010	36	69	270	375
TOTAL	**14,602**	**5,986**	**22,442**	**43,030**

SOURCE Derived from figures given on South Asia Terrorism Portal at: http://www.satp.org/satporgtp/countries/india/states/jandk/data_sheets/annual_casualties.htm provide a clear picture of the changes in the level of violence since the insurgency began.

Unimplemented Solutions

Hitherto in this chapter the focus has been on the methods that states have used to promote political accommodation and on the outcome of their efforts. However, it is also worth considering cases where these different modes of accommodation have been advocated but have not – at least not yet – been implemented. For example, to take the case just described, it has long been contended that autonomy will form a key element in any solution to the Kashmiri problem, especially since the failure of India to grant autonomy to the state was one of the factors that fuelled Kashmiri alienation from India in the first place. Robert Wirsing concurs that autonomy is likely to feature in the area's political future, but he argues that progress towards such a solution requires the transformation of relations between India and Pakistan, not as part of the settlement process but in advance of it (Wirsing 2004: 98).

Just as the two-state solution has dominated discourse on the settlement of the Israeli–Palestinian conflict, the formula of a bi-zonal, bi-communal federation has dominated consideration of the Cyprus problem for two decades. It formed the basis of the Annan plan that Greek Cypriot voters rejected in a referendum in 2004. Notwithstanding this setback, the formula has remained the basis for the internationally sponsored negotiations that have continued to take place between the parties. In the case of Sri Lanka, which was engulfed in a long-running civil war between July 1983 and May 2009, proposals for the autonomy of the Tamil North were put forward at an early stage, as a response to the demand of the Liberation Tigers of Tamil Eelam (LTTE) for independence. The war went through a number of phases, and there were a number of efforts to achieve a negotiated settlement in the course of the conflict. The most substantial effort to conclude the war through negotiations involved Norwegian mediation and followed a LTTE ceasefire in 2002. Also mooted during these negotiations was that there should be power-sharing at the national level to ensure Tamil participation in the government of Sri Lanka in what amounted to a consociational approach. After the breakdown of these negotiations, the LTTE abandoned its ceasefire and there was a resumption of the war. It ended in May 2009 with the LTTE's complete defeat. In its aftermath, the government's priority was to capitalise politically on the popularity it had secured among the Sinhala majority as a result of its military victory. It presented its victory as a triumph over terrorism, a representation that could be readily justified with reference to the methods the LTTE had used during the war. It had little need politically to seek to conciliate the Tamil minority.

Events in Sri Lanka contradict the assumption that violent conflict in deeply divided societies can only be ended by negotiations leading to a settlement that is based on principles for the political accommodation of the communities caught up in the conflict. However, to acknowledge that violent conflicts may end in the victory of one side or the other (and more commonly of the government rather than of the insurgents) is not to accept the desirability of such outcomes. But it is salutary to consider the political obstacles that stand in the way of settlements designed to accommodate diversity of one kind or another. And these may include the fact that one or other of the parties may choose the pursuit of a military victory, whether attainable or not. In this context it should also be acknowledged that insurgents are not always representative of the community on whose behalf they claim to be fighting. Governments can legitimately argue that, according the political representatives of insurgents, a place in the negotiations on a new constitutional dispensation rewards their violence. But the desirability of an end to violent conflict during the course of negotiations may override this objection.

In his writings on consociationalism Lijphart stresses the crucial role of political will in the achievement of consociational democracy. He argues that this factor may prove more important in determining the feasibility of such democracy than the presence or the absence of all the favourable conditions for consociationalism that he outlines. It is a fundamental point. Few governments readily give up or share political power. That may do more to explain the current relative rarity of consociational democracies or of ethnic federations than their unsuitability in a world in which globalisation has increased the importance of identity politics, and hence the need for the recognition of diversity to be reflected much more widely in the construction of countries' political institutions. Only *in extremis* do governments contemplate such fundamental changes. The exceptions tend to be cases where the country is already going through a major transformation or following the breakdown of the previous regime. External involvement may also be a facilitating factor. The role of external parties in addressing the problems of deeply divided societies is examined in the next chapter.

8 EXTERNAL MEDIATION

The violence associated with deeply divided societies and the possibility of spill-over effects, such as an exodus of refugees or the spread of conflict to neighbouring states, mean that the problems of deeply divided societies inevitably have significant international implications. But such societies constitute a challenge to the global political order in a number of ways, beyond simply their association with violent conflict that disturbs the peace of the world. Since conflicts in deeply divided societies reflect an absence of consensus and polarisation over how the society should be governed, they tend to revolve around contested interpretations of fundamental political principles. A disaffected community that rejects the legitimacy of the existing mechanisms for decision-making in a society typically seeks to couch its objections in terms of universally recognised norms. Commonly in dispute, in many conflicts, is the application of the principle of self-determination to the particular situation. This point is strongly emphasised by Christine Bell in her analysis of peace agreements in the 1990s, which is centred on the cases of South Africa, Northern Ireland, Israel/Palestine and Bosnia-Herzegovina. She argues that a characteristic of the agreements reached in the 1990s in the four cases she highlights was that they 'attempted to address the self-determination claims at the heart of the conflict' (Bell 2000: 119).

The issue of self-determination has been given added importance by the implicit changes in its interpretation that have taken place since the end of the Cold War. These changes occurred in part – but not wholly – as a consequence of the international community's adjustment to political developments in Eastern Europe and the former Soviet Union. The unacknowledged nature of the changes reflects the lack of an international consensus on reformulating the norm. At the same time, the increase in the number of independent states that has occurred since 1990 has given impetus to external mediation to address the potentially destabilising implications of changing international boundaries. And, in tandem with the perceived need for external mediation in the conflicts that have arisen over self-determination disputes, there has been a further erosion of the non-intervention norm, so that the circumstances in which major powers have justified their intervention in other states have multiplied.

Self-Determination

To get to grips with these issues more fully, a brief history of the norm of self-determination is instructive. Like the notion of popular sovereignty, self-determination was associated with the French and American revolutions at the end of the eighteenth century. In particular, once the idea had taken root that the people, as citizens, were entitled to determine how they were ruled, the question quite naturally arose as to whether they wished to be part of a particular state, even if that had potentially massively disruptive implications. However, the principle of self-determination really came fully into its own during the course of the First World War, when it was championed by the Western powers. Their proclamation of the rights of the small nationalities of Eastern Europe owed much to their appreciation of its likely impact on the multi-national empires they were at war with. The element of hypocrisy in this appeal was highlighted in a note from the Habsburg Empire in January 1917.

> If the adversaries demand above all the restoration of invaded rights and liberties, the recognition of the principle of nationalities and of the free existence of small states, it will suffice to call to mind the tragic fate of the Irish and Finnish peoples, the obliteration of the freedom and independence of the Boer Republics, the subjection of North Africa by Great Britain, France and Italy, and, lastly, the violence brought to bear on Greece for which there is no precedent in history. (Cobban 1969: 49–50)

The person most closely associated with the principle of national self-determination, as it was then formulated, was the president of the United States, Woodrow Wilson. He made implementation of the principle of national self-determination a fundamental part of the Allies' war aims in his fourteen points and four principles of January 1918. The use of the term 'national' defined those entitled to self-determination as the collective members of a nation, but it begged the further question of who constituted a nation. A combination of linguistic and cultural criteria were employed for this purpose. They proved lethal to Eastern Europe's multi-national empires. Given the complex ethnic mosaic in the area, the potential for division was almost limitless. What held the process of disintegration in check were old-fashioned power considerations; so, in practice, ethnic lines of division were often overridden in determining the boundaries of the new states.

Some of the new boundaries were decided through plebiscites, but inevitably minorities remained however the boundaries were drawn. The issue of the treatment of minorities became a major preoccupation of the League of Nations. The principal device to protect minorities after the end of the First World War was the insertion into the peace treaties of clauses on minority rights so that 'in one way or another every one of the lesser states of Central and Eastern Europe compulsorily or voluntarily undertook to guarantee certain rights to its minorities' (Cobban 1969: 87). However, the imposition of such obligations remained bitterly resented and the limited commitments states entered into were poorly honoured. But the disparity between practice and principle was less important than the fact that the very existence of the principle was a potent weapon in the hands of anyone wishing to advance irredentist claims. In particular, there were German minorities scattered across Eastern Europe and deep into the Soviet Union for Hitler to champion.

Outstanding among these was the case of the Sudeten Germans in Western Czechoslovakia. Czechoslovakia had been constructed on the highly contestable principle that the Czechs and Slovaks constituted a single people. Even on this assumption, others made up more than a third of the country's population. It was child's play for Hitler to use the principle of national self-determination, as it had been proclaimed by President Wilson, to destroy the country (Tolland 1997: 511–20). After the Second World War there was a determination that no great power should be allowed to use the lever of minority rights in another country to further its own ambitions. The result was a de-emphasis on minority or group rights of any kind. Instead the United Nations (UN) stressed the principle of individual human rights.

At the same time, national self-determination became simply self-determination. Peoples rather than nations were seen as having the right to self-determination, and 'people' was defined simply as the inhabitants of a territory. In short, the criterion for determining who was entitled to self-determination was no longer ethnic or cultural, but territorial. This new criterion was appropriate for the process of decolonisation the world was embarking upon, since it established the principle that decolonisation should take place within existing colonial boundaries, placing constraints on what was otherwise a revolutionary change within the international political system. It also put an end to the notion that some prior claim to nationhood was a pre-condition for the assertion of a right to self-determination. During the process of decolonisation itself, the new interpretation of the principle of self-determination met with a measure of opposition from colonial powers wishing to retain control of parts of their empire. Thus, it was virtually at the end of the process of decolonisation that the international community, through the United Nations General Assembly, set down in definitive terms its understanding of the principle of self-determination in the 1970 *Declaration of Principles of International Law concerning Friendly Relations and Co-operation among States in accordance with the Charter of the United Nations*. One of the most important aspects of the section on self-determination was its rejection of the notion of secession from an independent state. This section concluded:

> Nothing in the foregoing paragraphs shall be construed as authorizing or encouraging any action which would dismember or impair, totally or in part, the territorial integrity or political unity of sovereign and independent States conducting themselves in compliance with the principle of equal rights and self-determination and thus possessed of a government representing the whole people belonging to the territory without distinction as to race, creed, or colour.
>
> Every State shall refrain from any action aimed at the partial or total disruption of the national unity and territorial integrity of any other State or country. (General Assembly Resolution 2625 of 1970: 124)

During the 1960s the international community demonstrated its opposition to secession in two important cases in Africa. Belgium's large colony in Central Africa, the Congo, became independent at the end of June 1960. Eleven days later the south-eastern province of Katanga proclaimed its independence from the new state, a secession that was to last until January 1963. Katanga's secession was supported by a broad alliance of forces, including settlers, in what was by far the richest province of the Congo by virtue of its mineral wealth. The secession of Katanga was not the only problem that the new state faced. A mutiny in the Congolese army had immediately followed independence, prompting Belgian military intervention. The UN responded to the breakdown of law and order in the Congo by embarking on an ambitious exercise in peace-keeping. The question of what the Organisation des Nations Unies au Congo (ONUC) was entitled to do under its mandate was a matter of controversy. Leading figures in ONUC, such as the Irish diplomat Conor Cruise O'Brien, took the view that upholding the Congo's territorial integrity justified the use of UN

troops to end Katanga's secession (Cruise O'Brien 1962). This angered the
supporters of the Katangese leader Moise Tshombe, who included right-
wing opinion in the West impressed by Tshombe's anti-communism, as
well as white settlers in Central and Southern Africa.

The other major episode of secession was that of Biafra from Nigeria.
Nigeria became an independent state in October 1960. It was a federation
of three large regions. The country's democratic institutions survived to
January 1966, when there was a military coup. The coup's leaders were
associated with the eastern region, the homeland of the Ibos. The threat
of the imposition of a unitary system on the country prompted a second
military coup in July 1966, this time led by northerners. Many Ibo army
officers were murdered in the course of the coup, and the coup itself was
followed by mob violence against Ibos who had migrated to the northern
region. These circumstances might have been sufficient by themselves to
have prompted secession. A further factor was the Eastern region's immense
resources of oil, which were just beginning to be exploited. The region
seceded from Nigeria under the name 'Biafra', on 30 May 1967. Civil war
followed, which ended with Biafra's capitulation on 12 January 1970.

France's attitude towards Biafra was sympathetic, but generally speaking Biafra was unable to attract support from other states. In particular, the
federal government of Nigeria was aided during the course of the war by
both Britain and the Soviet Union, which made it a rather unusual case of
co-operation across the Iron Curtain during the Cold War (Mayall 1971:
159–64). Sympathy for Biafra's cause was at its peak during 1969, when
extensive starvation within the territory attracted the attention of a number
of non-governmental organisations. However, even this humanitarian
emergency did not turn the tide of world opinion in Biafra's favour.
Further, relatively little weight was given to the question of how much
support there was for secession in Biafra. Few doubted at this time that
Biafra's charismatic leader, Colonel Ojukwu, enjoyed the backing of a
majority of Ibos. Opponents of Biafra's secession stressed the destabilising
consequences for the whole of the African continent, if the independence
of Biafra was allowed to stand.

Challenges to the Post-Colonial Norm

Ironically, shortly after the international community had endorsed the 1970
Declaration, circumstances arose that undercut its absolute anathema to
secession. Elections in Pakistan in December 1970 resulted in victory
for the Awami League, which called for Pakistan to be governed as
a loose confederation. It had overwhelming support in the east wing of

the country. In the face of this demand, the Pakistani political elite based in the west wing of the country opted to use the army, in an attempt to suppress the Awami League. The Awami League responded by declaring the secession of the east wing from Pakistan in April 1971. The resistance of the west wing to the establishment of Bangladesh lasted until December 1971. Decisive to the victory of the secessionists was India's intervention in their support. The United States government strongly opposed the secession, citing the 1970 Declaration in support of its position. However, while its naval forces were deployed to underline its position, the United States did not intervene directly in the conflict. The acceptance of Bangladesh into the international community was not followed by any reconsideration of the 1970 Declaration. Bangladesh was rationalised as a special case, for three reasons. Pakistan had been a product of partition. Its east and west wings had been separated by hundreds of miles. The people in the east wing wishing to secede actually constituted a majority in the country as a whole.

A much greater challenge to the norm arose as a consequence of the demise of communism in Eastern Europe and in the Soviet Union at the end of the 1980s and the beginning of the 1990s. Initially, an attempt was made by leading Western powers such as the United States to fit the changes taking place as a result of the collapse of communism within the framework of existing international norms. The West had no stake in the survival of a democratic Soviet Union and there was a pre-existing commitment to recognise the independence of the three Baltic republics of Latvia, Estonia and Lithuania, as they had once been members of the League of Nations. But the attempt was made to hold the rest together, at least notionally, under the umbrella of the Commonwealth of Independent States (CIS). The government of Georgia was ostracised by the West for a period because it tried to stay out of the CIS. However, in the end, the CIS framework failed to achieve credibility, and independent states emerged in each of the former constituent republics of the Soviet Union. In fact the threat of disintegration did not stop there; there were numerous challenges to the legitimacy of the new states from disaffected communities and regions, most notably in the case of the Russian Federation from Chechnya, until Putin, prime minister and then president, ended Russian equivocation over the status of Chechnya.

While the disintegration of the Soviet Union might have been rationalised as the belated dissolution of the tsarist empire, no such rationalisation was available in the case of the breakup of Yugoslavia, since the former Yugoslavia was itself a product of the collapse of the Austro-Hungarian Empire. The American government opposed both Slovenia's and Croatia's unilateral declarations of independence in June 1991.

However, at the end of the year Germany recognised the new secessionist entities. Other members of the European Community followed suit, paving the way for their general international recognition and membership of the United Nations. This happened despite widespread inter-communal violence in Croatia, which was fuelled by the Serbian minority's fear of Croatian ethno-nationalism. The Serb response was underpinned by the provocative adoption, by Croatian nationalists, of the symbols of the war-time Croatian state, which had been responsible for the mass killings of Serbs. The old Yugoslavia consisted of six republics and, in an attempt to give the appearance of even-handedness and rationality to its Balkan policies, the European Community offered the choice of independence to the other four. The choice of independence, made by Bosnia-Herzegovina's multi-ethnic society in circumstances of political mobilisation along ethnic lines, produced the predictable outcome of civil war. Faced by rapid political change and uncertainty as to where authority for decision-making would ultimately rest, people in the former Yugoslavia fell back on ethnic solidarity as offering their best hope for some measure of security. However, since where ethnic groups lived did not coincide neatly with the pre-existing territorial divisions of the country, the consequence was conflict among the communities and attempts to make territory and ethnicity coincide through the practice of ethnic cleansing.

The disintegration of Yugoslavia did not stop at the level of federal units. The country's ethnic diversity was reflected in the lower levels of government. The most significant case was that of Kosovo. The majority of the population of the region was Albanian in ethnic terms. Pro-independence demonstrations took place in the region as far back as 1968. In an attempt to accommodate the ethnic Albanians, Tito made Kosovo an autonomous province of Serbia in 1974. However, following conflict between the ethnic Albanians and the Serb minority in the province, Kosovo had been stripped of its autonomy in the late 1980s. This was not accepted by the ethnic Albanian community, which embarked upon a campaign of passive resistance to Serbian rule. After the secession of Slovenia and Croatia, the ethnic Albanians argued that the Yugoslav federation was dead and that they owed the rump state of Yugoslavia no loyalty. However, only Albania recognised their declaration of independence. During the course of the Bosnian conflict there had been periodic fears of an eruption in Kosovo. However, despite a high level of tension, the region remained outwardly peaceful until the emergence of the Kosovo Liberation Army in 1996.

After the killing of Serbian police officers in February 1998 and extensive reprisals by the Serbian security forces, there was a serious escalation in inter-communal violence during the summer of 1998, with the Kosovo

Liberation Army (KLA) seizing control of a large proportion of the region, followed by a counter-offensive by the Serbs. A UN Security Council resolution called for a ceasefire. Under the threat of North Atlantic Treaty Organization (NATO) air strikes, the Serbian President, Slobodan Milošević, agreed to a withdrawal of Serbian troops and to the stationing of monitors to verify his government's compliance with NATO's demands. However, when this unsurprisingly failed to break the cycle of inter-communal violence, Serbian compliance ceased. As Western governments possessed neither the means nor, as importantly, the disposition to control the activities of the KLA, every fresh cycle of violence simply prompted ever greater demands being made on the government of Serbia.

The point was finally reached, in negotiations on a peace settlement at Rambouillet in February and March 1999, that NATO was threatening to bomb Serbia unless it agreed to permit a referendum on the unilateral secession of Kosovo from Serbia after a transition period in which Kosovo would be governed as a NATO protectorate. Given the history of the region, there was never any prospect that any government in Belgrade could have voluntarily agreed to such terms and survived. NATO military intervention followed, in order to end Serbia's control of the region. After an aerial campaign that included the bombing of installations in Belgrade, it achieved complete Serbian withdrawal in June 1999. There was then a period of international supervision of the government of the territory under the authority of the United Nations. After the failure of negotiations on the status of the region, Kosovo declared its independence in February 2008. However, many countries have declined to recognise the new state.

Two cases of secession in Africa since the end of the Cold War warrant consideration. In 1993 Eritrea seceded from Ethiopia. Two factors limited the implications of this case for other societies. Firstly, the secession was by mutual agreement of the parties. Secondly, Eritrea's independence could be seen as the belated implementation of an important principle of the well-established post-colonial norm of self-determination, which was that territories that had been ruled as colonies were entitled to independence within those boundaries. Thus it could be argued that, as a former colony of Italy, Eritrea had always been entitled to its own separate independence. Difficulty has arisen over the issue of the new state's boundaries. Eritrea's border dispute with Ethiopia, which resulted in hostilities between 1998 and 2000, remains unresolved. Neither side has been willing to implement the proposals put forward by the United Nations border commission in 2002 to settle the dispute.

The other African case is that of South Sudan. As part of the 2002 peace deal that ended the long-running war between the south and the central government in Khartoum, it was agreed that the people in the south would be allowed to choose whether they wanted a separate state in a referendum in January 2011. The outcome of the referendum was a massive vote by southerners in favour of independence – a choice partially underpinned by the region's oil reserves, which promise a more prosperous future for its people than their poverty-stricken past. Again, it might be argued in this case that no precedent has been set, since the creation of a new state was the product of agreement among the parties, of which there were a number of previous examples – such as Singapore's secession from the Malaysian Federation, which took place even before the end of the Cold War.

However, there remains the further complication in Sudan's case of the revolt in Darfur in response to the deal between the central government and the south, which puts in question the stability and durability of the new division of political authority. The role that external parties and external pressure have played in negotiations on the future of Sudan provides an added dimension of controversy. The referendum paved the way for South Sudan to become the world's newest state on 11 July 2011. A feature of the period between the referendum and the day of independence was fighting between the Sudanese forces and those of the south over the border region of Abyei, the destiny of which had not been determined by the referendum. A feature of the conflict there, with similarities to the situation in Darfur, was that it followed the lines of a fault line between cultivators and pastoralists.

Another new state to emerge after 1990, indirectly as a result of the end of the Cold War, was East Timor. Timor was a relatively rare instance of an island that had been colonised by two states. East Timor was a colony of Portugal, while the rest of the island was part of the Dutch East Indies. Portugal, unlike the other European powers, hung onto its overseas empire until the 1970s and its own revolution in 1974. In terms of the post-colonial norm of self-determination, East Timor was entitled to its own separate independence. After the Portuguese withdrew their administration, divisions among the populace on the territory's constitutional future prompted a brief civil war out of which the principal nationalist movement emerged victorious. It proclaimed the territory's independence in November 1975. The following month Indonesia invaded and annexed East Timor.

Indonesia justified its actions as preventing a communist takeover of the territory that could prove a springboard for causing regional instability. Despite the huge loss of life that followed Indonesia's invasion and decimated the territory's population, international opposition to the takeover remained relatively muted. Indonesia did not secure wide recognition of its annexation, but at the same time East Timor's cause was not strongly supported even in the United Nations General Assembly. The end of the Cold War changed attitudes towards the issue and removed the geo-strategic reason for Western acquiescence in Indonesia's continuing occupation. As a consequence, the volume of criticism of Indonesia's brutal conduct in the territory went up markedly. However, it was internal developments in Indonesia rather than the international campaign on behalf of East Timor that was the catalyst for change (Westmoreland 2009: xxii). The Asian financial crisis was instrumental in bringing about the fall of the Suharto dictatorship in 1998 (McCloskey 2000: 9). Despite opposition in the military, the new Indonesian government decided that it needed a quick solution to the problem of East Timor to prevent the issue from contributing to a wider process of disintegration. It first offered East Timor autonomy, then a choice between autonomy and independence. The circumstances of Indonesia's rapid withdrawal were not propitious for the new state, as Cordell and Wolff explain:

> [T]he UN-administered referendum for independence in East Timor in 1999 was accompanied by massive intimidation and violence of the East Timorese by Indonesian regular and irregular forces, which further increased once the results (a clear vote for independence) were made public. As a consequence, some 200,000 people were forced to flee. Moreover, as a result of the destruction that occurred at this time, what little infrastructure East Timor possessed was all but destroyed, and most of the better educated residents, who were overwhelmingly non-Timorese, withdrew with the Indonesian forces. For a variety of reasons, some of which are not in any substantive way related to the period of occupation, to this day East Timor, although independent, barely functions as a state. (Cordell and Wolff 2009: 176–7)

Regardless of the special factors that have played a role in the creation of new states since the end of the Cold War, the cumulative impact has been to erode the strong anathema to secession that was contained in the 1970 declaration of the United Nations on self-determination quoted above. As a consequence, a powerful boost has been given to ethno-nationalist movements seeking independence for their homelands. It is by no means the only factor contributing to ethno-nationalist mobilisation since 1990. The trend away from the politics of class and of redistribution towards politics focused on issues of identity has facilitated ethno-nationalism. Globalisation too has had a paradoxical effect in assisting the cause of secession by undermining the contention that size matters for economic viability. In this context, the opportunities for small states to become members of regional economic blocs have also reduced the force of such arguments.

The New Interventionism

The enhanced prospects for secession are also connected to the erosion of the non-intervention norm. Changing attitudes towards the norm are reflected in the growth in the influence of such doctrines of intervention as the responsibility to protect and humanitarian intervention. The premise of responsibility to protect is that there is an onus on the international community to intervene in situations where the lives of a country's civilian population are threatened by the actions of government. In this context 'humanitarian intervention' means military action intended to affect the course of a conflict, and not the less contentious actions of humanitarian agencies in seeking to alleviate the impact of conflict on civilian populations. Admittedly, the sway of these doctrines is by no means universal. Support for these justifications of intervention is strongest in the West, particularly in the media. And their influence has been most apparent in the conduct of the foreign policy of major Western powers, which is not to argue that they have overridden the primacy of strategic interests in the responses of Western states to conflicts in other societies. But simply the possibility that major powers might be responsive to the argument that the world should not stand idly by in the face of a humanitarian emergency has provided encouragement to groups challenging the status quo through violence, including separatists seeking to change the boundaries of the state.

Ideas such as responsibility to protect are by no means the only reason for the increasing number of cases of military intervention since the end of the Cold War. Other factors have been at least as significant. Prior to 1990 a significant constraint on Western intervention in internal conflicts in the Third World was fear of Soviet counter-intervention. The dissolution of the Soviet Union eliminated this factor. While Russia continues to be regarded as a weak rival of the West in geo-strategic terms, its capacity to project power remains very limited. Admittedly in 2008 Russian support for South Ossetia and Abkhazia played a decisive role in preventing the forcible reincorporation of these enclaves into Georgia. The revolution in military technology has also played a part, giving confidence to Western planners that the military objectives of intervention can be achieved at a relatively low cost. Further, the circumstances of the collapse of communism in Eastern Europe have given confidence to the belief, in the major Western powers, that democracy, human rights and the rule of law have such universal appeal that intervention directed at establishing political dispensations that embody these values will be supported within the target state.

Even the difficulties that the United States and other states supporting these missions have encountered in Iraq and Afghanistan have not fundamentally shaken these assumptions. Indeed, the Arab Spring in 2011, notwithstanding some concerns over the role Islamists have played in fomenting opposition to the autocrats, was widely interpreted as a Middle Eastern version of 1989, and it was assumed that it would have the same result of replacing dictatorships with liberal democracies. When the revolt spread to Colonel Gaddafi's Libya and the regime's response was the suppression of the protests by military means, calls for military intervention to protect the civilian population followed, leading ultimately to the authorisation of military action by the United Nations Security Council. From the outset, France, Britain and the United States made it clear that they saw Gaddafi's removal from power as a necessary aspect of the mission, but there was limited endorsement of this view in the rest of the world. Nonetheless, the readiness of Western powers to seek regime change in this case suggests that interventions of a similar sort cannot be ruled out in the future when the opportunity arises and it seems likely that the opponents of pariah regimes will seek to test the limits of Western preparedness to intervene on the basis of the responsibility to protect.

External Engagement

External involvement in conflicts in deeply divided societies takes a wide variety of forms. And it may include a wide range of different actors, state and non-state. In the case of ethnic conflicts, diasporas of the ethnic groups involved in the conflict frequently contribute funds, and even arms, to the community they identify with, through organisations they see as representing the aspirations of the group in question. There is a tendency among diasporas to give their support to militant organisations as the most uncompromising advocates of the community's aspirations. Examples are the contributions that Irish Americans made to the Provisional Irish Republican Army (IRA) during the course of Northern Ireland's troubles and the support from the Tamil diaspora that the Tamil Tigers were able to tap. Admittedly, in the former case, the sums of money raised for the IRA were very small, especially in relation to the number of people in the United States who identified themselves in censuses as Irish Americans. But the contribution made was significant in the context of the scale of the IRA's operations and Northern Ireland's small population. Another concern in relation to diasporas is that militant elements in the diaspora will resort to terrorism outside the arena of conflict, thereby providing a global dimension to a local or regional conflict.

It is worth emphasising that, in general, external interest in conflict in a deeply divided society can have malign rather than benign consequences. There is a strong human disposition towards partisanship in cases of violent conflict. The impetus for external involvement quite commonly stems from identification of one side of the conflict as victims and the other as perpetrators. In the process, the distinction that should be made between current political leaders, who may be obdurate and uncompromising, and the communities they seek to represent tends to be lost sight of. Such judgements are especially dangerous when the prospect of establishing any durable peace depends on a settlement that is sufficiently balanced to be capable of securing and retaining support across the divide in a society. An evident difficulty is the derision that tends to be heaped on notions of balance or of impartiality in current political discourse.

International intervention in Libya provides a striking case in point. Hostility towards Colonel Gaddafi over the past involvement of Libya in transnational terrorism, coupled with concern over the fate of civilians challenging his rule, initially blinded both the media and policymakers in the West to the larger political significance of the country's regional divisions. This issue was well brought out in a magazine article shortly after the start of NATO's intervention.

> The question that must now be asked is whether there will be enough centripetal force to keep Libya together. Today, the rebels protest that they have no intention of dividing the country and insist that tribal and provincial considerations are largely irrelevant. But the reality is that their movement is largely a Cyrenaican one, and that recruitment has taken place largely through tribal affiliation. Beyond a rejection of the Gaddafi regime, the Transitional National Council has given little indication of what its version of a post-Gaddafi Libya might look like. For his part, Gaddafi has rallied loyal tribes around him, and now relies on them for support more publicly than ever. With time, the historical Tripolitanian–Cyrenaican divide could gain new permanence. (El Amrani 2011: 20)

Admittedly, it is virtually inconceivable that the intervening powers would permit the partition of the country after regime change, but regional differences may well prove to be a source of future tensions and conflict.

A different problem may arise where external opinion finds it very difficult to identify one side as victims and the other as perpetrators, or where these categories seem to be constantly shifting, with atrocities being committed on all sides. An example is provided by the series of wars that have beset the Democratic Republic of the Congo since the collapse of the Mobutu regime. The carnage in these wars has dwarfed in scale anything that has happened anywhere else in the world, except for the genocide in neighbouring Rwanda. Séverine Autesserre has estimated that, in the decade before Joseph Kabila's inauguration as president of the Democratic Republic of Congo in 2006 brought a temporary respite from the killings, over 3 million Congolese had died in wars involving 'three Congolese rebel movements, 14 foreign armed groups and countless militias' (Autesserre 2008: 94).

Since the end of the Cold War, the focus in relation to external involvement in conflicts has primarily been on the role that external parties can play in resolving conflict. Particularly during the 1990s there was a shift from the part played by external parties in the fuelling of conflicts to their capacity to contribute, through mediation, to the ending of longstanding conflicts. The watershed in world affairs that came with the collapse of the communist system in Eastern Europe and in the Soviet Union appeared to have paved the way to an era of peace agreements. At the same time, the outbreak of new conflicts, particularly in the areas previously under communist rule, created fresh situations in which there appeared to be an urgent need for external mediation to put a cap on the violence and to prevent spill-over into other societies. In sharp contrast, during the years of the Cold War, internal conflicts tended to be seen as potential sites of competition between the superpowers. The fear was that, if one superpower became involved in support of one of the protagonists, then the other would be drawn in on the opposite side. This was seen as a possible first step in a ladder of escalation that might conceivably result in direct conflict between the superpowers themselves. That such situations should be avoided provided further underpinning for the non-intervention norm, especially given the fears that the end result of a military confrontation between the superpowers would be a nuclear conflagration. The end of bipolarity with the disappearance of the Soviet Union put an end to such concerns, particularly within the West. Consequently this reason for opposing intervention in internal conflicts evaporated.

Notwithstanding the normative injunctions against the involvement of the superpowers in internal conflicts, the fact that wars between states were relatively uncommon after the Second World War and boundaries relatively fixed in comparison with previous eras provided the powers with the motivation to influence the outcome of internal conflicts so as to advance their strategic interests. Consequently, a number of the world's internal conflicts were bound up with the Cold War system and inevitably profoundly affected by its demise. They provided an early opportunity for external mediation, to ensure that these conflicts were brought to a peaceful close. There are a considerable number of cases in which peace agreements were reached, with external assistance in one form or another. Examples in Africa include the Rome process involving the Catholic church, which paved the way to multi-party elections in Mozambique in 1993, and the Bicesse Accords of 1991, which ended the civil war in Angola. However, in Angola's case there was a resumption of the civil war after the opposition lost the 1992 elections – an outcome disputed by its leader, Jonas Savimbi. The renewed conflict only ended after Savimbi's death in 2002. During the Cold War, Angola's political divisions had been interpreted largely in ideological terms. The continuation of the civil war in the 1990s underscored the ethnic dimension of the country's divisions. In Latin America there were a number of externally mediated agreements ending conflicts between governments and left-wing insurgents, including in El Salvador, Guatemala and Colombia. Also a product of the end of the Cold War was a settlement of the Cambodian conflict. An international agreement paved the way to multi-party elections under United Nations supervision in 1993.

Even before the end of the Cold War, there were circumstances in which external involvement in internal conflicts could be justified, particularly if directed towards bringing the conflict to an end. This was where a case could be made that the conflict posed a threat to international peace and security. This was the rubric under which the United Nations Security Council could consider matters that might otherwise have been considered internal to the state and outside the remit of the organisation. Thus the argument that apartheid posed a threat beyond South Africa's borders provided the justification for international action through the United Nations on the issue. And, while initially the focus had been on Israel's conflict with Arab states, ultimately the relationship between Israelis and Palestinians came to be seen as the core of the problem and in its own right a legitimate subject of international attention. Admittedly, since Israel had avoided incorporating the Palestinians in the occupied territories into the country's body politic, the issue of their status in the long term had an international dimension that distinguished this case from conflicts where the citizenship of the protagonists was not in dispute.

Camp David and after

While establishing peace between Israel and Egypt was the main objective of the Camp David Agreement concluded under American mediation in 1978, it did address the position of the Palestinians by holding out the prospect for autonomous self-government for Palestinians in the occupied territories of the West Bank and Gaza. While little headway was made towards this objective prior to 1990, the principle had been established of American mediation in the conflict. Of the four cases that are the main focus of Christine Bell's book on peace agreements in the 1990s, the agreement on Israel/Palestine was the first to be achieved. The Declaration of Principles of September 1993 was the product of both American and Norwegian mediation. As the name of the agreement implied, it was by no means a comprehensive blueprint of a settlement, but simply a framework requiring considerable further negotiation between the parties to fill out the details.

Some progress was made in the mid-1990s with the establishment of the Palestinian Authority and the holding of elections among the Palestinians in the West Bank and Gaza that endorsed the stance of Palestinians who had supported the Oslo peace process, as it was widely dubbed in reference to the location of the negotiations that led up to the Declaration of Principles. But the larger hopes raised by the Oslo peace process were not fulfilled. Opposition on both sides, which manifested itself in political violence, undermined the promise of peace that was central to the accord's acceptance by Israel's Jewish majority, the dominant community in the conflict. The trust between the parties that was needed to make further headway in reaching agreements on implementation diminished. By the time of an American-led effort in 2000 to revive the process through negotiations at Camp David on a comprehensive settlement, expectations for success were low. The breakdown of these negotiations and sustained violence between the parties in the second half of 2000 and in 2001 and 2002 underlined the complete failure of the Oslo process. While there have been attempts to get the peace process back on track since the early 2000s, these efforts have been made more to deflect criticism that the West is indifferent to the continuation of the conflict than with any expectation of progress.

However, through the course of the 1990s, the ultimate failure of the Oslo peace process lay in the future. In the 1990s it remained an inspiration to others seeking an end to seemingly intractable conflicts, as well as an example of the benefits two different sorts of external mediation could bring. Norway provides an example of the mediator accepted as an intermediary by both sides of a conflict, on the basis of having no self-interested stake in the outcome of negotiations and of being without any capacity to coerce either of the parties. By contrast, the United States exemplifies the mediator that possesses leverage and the capacity to employ its resources to influence the stance of the parties. One society where the influence of the Oslo peace process was clearly apparent in the discourse both of commentators and protagonists in the conflict was Northern Ireland. In part, this arose out of comparisons that had been made during the 1980s when the Provisional IRA had invoked the examples of the armed struggles of the African National Congress and of the Palestine Liberation Organisation to give credibility to its long war strategy.

Northern Ireland's Long Peace

During the run up to the launch of the Northern Ireland peace process, with the issuing of a joint declaration by the British and Irish governments, the examples of the Middle East peace process and of the South African transition were constantly invoked by nationalists. They pressed this analogy to make the case for inclusive negotiations in which the political wing of the republican movement, Sinn Féin, would be represented, if not unconditionally, then following the abandonment of violence. This followed deadlock in the negotiations that had been confined to constitutional political parties – parties unconnected to organisations engaging in political violence. The joint declaration set out basic principles of a settlement, while offering Sinn Féin a place in the negotiations provided there was a permanent ceasefire by the Provisional IRA. Commentary following the joint declaration emphasised the influence of external events in making possible what was widely reported as a breakthrough in one of the world's most intractable conflicts. For example, *Le Monde* carried a cartoon showing John Major arm in arm with a hooded figure representing the IRA entering a café of peace where Rabin and Arafat and Mandela and De Klerk were already celebrating (Guelke 1994: 95–6).

In the event, the peace process proved a long one. Sinn Féin made clear that it rejected some aspects of the joint declaration. But the essential step to take the process forward was taken when the IRA announced an indefinite cessation of violence in August 1994. Unionists objected that this fell short of the permanent ceasefire required by the joint declaration. Delay in the start of negotiations among the parties then provided a pretext for the IRA to abandon its ceasefire in February 1996, with a bomb attack on Canary Wharf in London. This led to Sinn Féin's exclusion from the negotiations that followed, though not from the elections that preceded them. In the party's absence little progress was made. The following year, 1997, brought about changes of government in both London and Dublin and the IRA was persuaded to renew its ceasefire. The outcome was that Sinn Féin was able to enter the talks, though in response two unionist parties withdrew from the negotiations.

The process culminated in the Belfast Agreement of April 1998. Following its acceptance by the parties taking part in the negotiations, the accord was endorsed by substantial majorities in referendums in Northern Ireland and the Republic of Ireland. However, the overwhelming support of Catholics disguised the fact that only a narrow majority of Protestants had voted in favour of the deal. The implementation of the Belfast Agreement encountered many difficulties and at times its survival appeared to be in question. In the decade that followed the accord, Northern Ireland continued to be ruled from London under direct rule for most of the time, in the first place, because of the time it took to establish the devolved institutions, and in the second place, because of crises in the process that necessitated the suspension of the institutions. It required two further agreements to put the institutions on a firm foundation, the St Andrews Agreement of October 2006 and the Hillsborough Agreement of February 2010.

Throughout the different phases, from the joint declaration to the Hillsborough Agreement, a range of external parties was involved. Both the British and the Irish governments might be included in this category, since neither of the two represented any of the parties in Northern Ireland, though the British government had a constitutional responsibility for the governance of the province. The role of the two governments was central. They were largely responsible for drawing up both the Belfast and the St Andrews Agreements. Indeed, the Northern Ireland peace process may fairly be characterised as a case of external conflict management by the two governments. However, in addition, parties outside of Britain and Ireland played a more minor part in advancing the process. Three American administrations had an influence on the negotiations at critical junctures. President Clinton made three visits to Northern Ireland while in office. Significant steps taken by the Clinton administration included the grant of a short visa to Gerry Adams to visit the United States in January 1994, a decision supported by the Irish government but opposed by the British government, and Clinton's phone call to the leader of the Ulster Unionist Party, David Trimble, on 10 April 1998, urging him to accept the deal. President Bush also visited Northern Ireland. His visit in April 2003 was primarily a war summit on Iraq, but he also took the opportunity to support the efforts of the British and Irish government to revive the functioning of the power-sharing institutions under the Belfast Agreement. Though these efforts were unsuccessful, they did eventually pave the way after further sets of negotiations for the restoration of devolution in 2007. Behind the scenes, the Bush administration played a part in creating the conditions for this outcome by pressing Sinn Féin on the issues of policing and of crime. Similarly, in the crisis over the devolution of policing and justice powers in 2009–10, the Obama administration was prominent in urging unionists to accept the urgency of resolving the outstanding difficulties.

Factors that contributed to the influence of American administrations on the Northern Ireland peace process included the importance attached within Northern Ireland to attracting American investment in the economy and generally pro-American attitudes of the public on both sides of the sectarian divide in Northern Ireland. The latter, especially, made Northern Ireland untypical of most conflicts. The other country, outside of Britain and Ireland, that played a significant role in the Northern Ireland peace process was South Africa. Frequent comparison of South Africa and Northern Ireland, despite the vast differences between the two societies, meant that South Africa's transition was seen as offering hope that the intractable conflict in Northern Ireland might also be brought to an end through a negotiated settlement. The example was especially important to the leaders of the republican movement seeking to convince their followers that the end of the Provisional IRA's campaign without achieving a united Ireland was not a defeat. The African National Congress (ANC) was ready to assist in the process of persuasion, and its ties to the Labour Party in Britain and to Sinn Féin made it a trusted intermediary, which was reflected in the appointment of the ANC's chief negotiator as one of two international monitors of IRA arms dumps prior to the decommissioning of its weapons.

But also striking are the differences between the negotiating processes in South Africa and Northern Ireland. External parties did not play a prominent role in the negotiations that led to the country's transition to democracy. The key players throughout the process were the ANC and the National Party government. The fundamentally internal nature of the South African process mattered most for the National Party government, which regarded it as critical to the legitimacy of any agreement that was achieved. Its leaders contended that the fact that the parties freely agreed to the terms under which the country's first democratic elections took place helped to ensure the acceptance of the post-apartheid dispensation in the country. They also attached a lot of value to the preservation of constitutional continuity between the old and the new order. Key National Party figures, such as its chief negotiator, Roelf Meyer, downplayed the indirect influence of both outside pressures and external parties. This was reflected in Meyer's attitude towards negotiations in other conflicts. Thus, at the height of the crisis over implementation of the Belfast Agreement, Meyer urged the Northern Ireland parties to construct their own agreement, independently of both the British and the Irish governments.

Coercive Diplomacy

At the opposite end of the spectrum to South Africa was the manner in which the conflict in Bosnia-Herzegovina was brought to a close. The Dayton Peace Agreement of December 1995, both in the negotiation of its terms and in its implementation, epitomised coercive diplomacy (Burg 2003). Its objective was to preserve Bosnia-Herzegovina as a political entity. To this end a consociational constitution was imposed with the aim of forcing the internal political parties to co-operate. The accord was backed up by the stationing of an international military force to deter and, if necessary, to punish violations of the accord. The Office of the High Representative was created to oversee the implementation of the political provisions. The powers of the High Representative, who also served as the European Union (EU)'s special representative in Bosnia-Herzegovina, included the dismissal of elected representatives whose actions ran counter the Dayton Peace Agreement. Opinions of the Dayton Peace Agreement remain mixed, with critics claiming that the design of its political institutions entrenched ethnic divisions, as noted in the previous chapter. Weaknesses of the international intervention in the Balkans included both its partisanship and the pursuit of strategic advantage under the guise of humanitarianism, but mitigating these factors was the appeal of EU membership across the whole region. That prospect provided an incentive for governments of disparate make-ups to moderate their conduct.

Outside of the Balkans, coercive diplomacy has generally not proved an effective means of addressing the problems of deeply divided societies. Indeed, it can be argued that its use in one particular case contributed to the post-Cold War's greatest political catastrophe, the genocide in Rwanda. The Arusha Accords of August 1993, which external mediators pressurised the warring parties to accept, provided for power-sharing between the Rwandan government and the Rwandan Patriotic Front (RPF). The proposals were based on a conception of the conflict that was held by neither of the parties. The international community's interpretation of the conflict in ethnic terms ran contrary to the RPF's integrationist perspective, which rejected the designations of the population as an artificial construct of colonial divide and rule policies. It also went against the Rwandan government's very different conception of the conflict. From the perspective of its most extreme supporters, what the RPF was seeking to achieve was the re-enslavement of the Hutus under the hegemony of the Tutsis. The parties' rejection of the framework on which the proposals for power-sharing were based made it probable that either or both would defect from its terms when the opportunity arose. This likelihood was compounded by the reluctance of the members of the international community to commit resources or to put their military forces in harm's way in a situation in which they considered they had little or nothing at stake in strategic terms. That set the scene for the events of 1994, when the plane carrying the president of the country was shot down, triggering violence on a mass scale by Hutu militias.

Unremarkably, external mediation tends to work best in deeply divided societies when it is voluntarily accepted by the parties to the conflict. In circumstances in which one or other of the parties to a conflict rejects external mediation, it may seem tempting to overcome their resistance through external military intervention. But, as the cases of both Iraq and Afghanistan have underlined, it is very difficult for any occupying force to establish credible and effective political institutions if the legitimacy of its military intervention is rejected by a significant proportion of the population. The difficulties the major powers have encountered in these two cases stand in ironic contrast to the wave of demonstrations for democracy that swept North Africa in the early months of 2011. Fear of the consequences of continuing violence in terms of spill-over effects does provide a legitimate basis for external concern in other countries' internal conflicts and may constitute a justification for intervention. But, in the case of deeply divided societies, the consequences of intervention are likely to prove problematic at best.

9 CONCLUSION

Political conditions in deeply divided societies vary, and deeply divided societies themselves take many different forms. In some, the divisions are vertical in character; in others horizontal. And, though deeply divided societies tend to be associated with intractable violent political conflicts, this is not a permanent condition or necessarily a reliable yardstick as to whether a deeply divided society exists. And deeply divided societies do come and go, which is not to argue that, once a fault line has become entrenched in any society, it can easily be overcome. Reference has been made to circumstances in which new deeply divided societies may come into existence, such as the settlement of people from the dominant ethnic group in a peripheral region, in order to secure its attachment to the centre. And considerable attention has been given to the topic of reaching agreements in deeply divided societies so as to bring an end to violent conflict. However, the stopping of violent conflict does not necessarily mean an end to deep divisions in society. Indeed, a characteristic of deeply divided societies is that they may enjoy long periods of tranquillity, in which there is a truce between the major factions in the society but the fault line remains. The vulnerability of such a society to renewed violent conflict may not even be apparent, and the resurfacing of the old divisions may come as a shock to all concerned. The ethnic conflicts that engulfed the Balkans after the collapse of communism provide an obvious example, though there remains plenty of scope for debate as to how far the conflicts were the product of entirely new circumstances and how far they represented a revival of old rivalries that had remained frozen under communist rule.

But, while violence plays an important role in deeply divided societies in helping to create a force field, the violence remains a reflection or symptom of conflict at a deeper level. Hence the argument has been put forward that what is fundamental to deeply divided societies is contested legitimacy. It is worth dwelling, in this context, on the importance of legitimate political institutions to any society, and also on the problem of judging whether a society's political institutions are legitimate in the eyes of its populace. The events across North Africa and in the Middle East in 2011 have underlined that the previous outward appearance of political stability of many of the countries across the Arab world was deceptive. Yet it might also be a mistake to conclude that regimes which have succumbed to popular revolts were never legitimate at any stage in their existence. It is tempting to argue that the universal appeal of liberal democracy provides a justification for regarding regimes that are not the product of regular free elections as suspect in terms of their legitimacy. At the same time, the holding of free elections does not itself guarantee the creation of long-lasting legitimate institutions. Thus there are few societies in the world in which there have never been countrywide democratic elections, though these do include the important case of China. However, many of the world's authoritarian regimes have emerged out of the breakdown of liberal democracies.

The Quest for Legitimacy

A general indication that a government is legitimate is the routine acceptance of its authority by the population. This does not preclude debate and disagreement over policy questions or the mobilisation of opinion against particular government policies. However, in situations in which the government's legitimacy is accepted, the enforcement of its decisions, however unpopular, will generally not encounter violent opposition. The more a government has to rely overtly on coercion to enforce its will, the less legitimate it is likely to appear. Creating and maintaining legitimate political institutions is a challenge for any society. Admittedly, in well-established democracies the existence of legitimate political institutions tends to be taken for granted, to the extent that it may be difficult for the citizens of such societies fully to appreciate the obstacles in other societies to institutionalising procedures for decision-making capable of securing widespread acceptance. The predisposition of the electorate in a politically stable liberal democracy to expect the basic rules for the functioning of its institutions to continue to be followed is for the most part an asset. However, it may lead to complacency about the durability of democratic institutions in changing circumstances. Deeply divided societies face the opposite problem. Past conflicts cast a long shadow over their efforts to entrench legitimate political institutions. It is rarely, if ever, possible for people in deeply divided societies to take for granted success in putting into place a political dispensation that removes any possibility of renewed conflict.

Given the characterisation of deeply divided societies as polities in which there is a contest for legitimacy between mutually incompatible political projects, it might seem axiomatic that they would encounter extreme difficulty in overcoming their divisions. This logic is evident in Bernard Crick's assessment of the prospects for South Africa, Israel/ Palestine and Northern Ireland in his keynote address at a conference on these three cases in Bonn in 1989. Crick stated:

> I call the three problems 'insoluble' for two formal reasons: (i) that no internal solution likely to guarantee peace can possibly satisfy the announced principles of the main disputants and (ii) that any external imposed solution or enforced adjudication is likely to strengthen the desperation and self-righteousness of the threatened group (Crick 1990: 265).

But, while the description of the conflict in Israel/Palestine as insoluble still seems relevant, South Africa and Northern Ireland have changed fundamentally since 1989, in a manner that belies Crick's assumptions and requires explanation.

In the midst of conflict in which the parties pursue what they see as legitimate objectives, while denying the legitimacy of the other side's objectives, it often seems as if conflict can only end in the event of the victory of one side or the other. The propaganda of the protagonists may encourage such a belief through its emphasis on the unacceptability of compromise. Thus, according to a trite witticism, problems have solutions, but conflicts only have winners and losers. In fact the presentation of any situation in such zero-sum terms has obvious advantages for those seeking to mobilise support for violent action likely to entail considerable costs. This is most likely to happen if the path to reform seems blocked. Quite commonly conflicts follow a pattern of rapid escalation from small beginnings until the violence reaches a peak. If no side has won by this stage, there tends to be a decline from the peak towards a plateau. For example, in Northern Ireland violence rose from street disturbances in 1968 to a peak in 1972, when nearly five hundred people died as a result of the troubles. The level of violence fell in the late 1970s to average under a hundred deaths a year for the remainder of the troubles, up to the paramilitary ceasefires of 1994, as Table 4.2 in Chapter 4 shows.

Negotiated Settlements

For political mobilisation in support of goals such as the creation of a new state, the merger into another state or the establishment of a new political dispensation to be successful, the objectives need to accord with the aspirations of a large proportion of the community being appealed to. However, this does not mean that communities, whether defined in terms of ethnicity, religious belief or class, are incapable of adjusting to the circumstances they face. They may accept political arrangements that fall well short of the full achievement of their aspirations for the sake of an end to the conflict, particularly if they are persuaded that their interests will be protected under a new dispensation negotiated between the parties. But readiness to agree to such a deal may take considerable time and only be reached after a prolonged period of stalemate. The point is well reflected in Zartman's writings on negotiations, in which he puts considerable emphasis on the issue of timing as providing a key element in achieving the peaceful resolution of conflicts.

> While most studies on peaceful settlements of disputes see the substance of the proposals as the key to a successful resolution of conflict, a growing focus of attention shows that a second and equally necessary key lies in the timing of efforts for resolution. Parties resolve their conflicts only when they are ready to do so – when alternative, usually unilateral, means of achieving a satisfactory result are blocked and the parties feel that they are in an uncomfortable and costly predicament. At that ripe moment, they grasp onto proposals that have usually been in the air for a long time and that only now appear attractive. (Zartman 2008: 22)

The difficulty remains that, if a mutually hurting stalemate persuades the parties to put aside the full achievement of goals that they continue to consider legitimate for the sake of peace, the suspicion may linger that the settlement is simply a truce and that, when the opportunity arises again, elements in one community or the other will resume the struggle for their original goals. That may be a factor in sustaining divisions after a negotiated settlement of the conflict. At the same time, changes in the external environment can and often do have a fundamental effect on the course both of conflicts and of peace processes. There are few places in Europe outside of Northern Ireland where sectarian differences within Christianity are still capable of sustaining social fault lines, as they more commonly did in the past. Thus, whereas issues of religion were once central to divisions in Belgium, language has replaced religion as the mainspring of that country's divide. Admittedly, contention over the presence of Muslim immigrants has become a political issue in a number of European countries. However, while there have been some ugly manifestations of islamophobia as a consequence, the deep division of any society simply on the question of Muslim immigration would seem unlikely to happen. The importance of class divisions tended to diminish in the decades following the end of the Cold War, but it may revive to a degree as a result of the global economic downturn.

One reason for believing that South Africa's divisions may gradually dissolve to the point that it is no longer possible to describe the country as a deeply divided society is that the hostility of the world towards racism practically rules out explicit mobilisation against the country's democratic dispensation on the basis of racial differences. Of course, that does not preclude the emergence of new fault lines in the society. However, there are few signs that ethnicity, for example, in the form of tribal identities is capable of playing the role that race once played in the country as a source of division, the legacy of which is still reflected in voting behaviour. By contrast, Northern Ireland's settlement is altogether more fragile than the irreversible change that has taken place in South Africa. Under the terms of the Belfast Agreement, nationalists have not given up their aspiration to achieve a united Ireland. Indeed, the accord provides a mechanism for the achievement of a united Ireland on the emergence of a majority in favour of such a step in Northern Ireland. Unionist acceptance of the accord is premised on the assumption that such a majority will not emerge. Each side has gambled that, in the long term, demographic developments will favour the achievement of its goals. While both cannot be right, it may be that the significance of the issue of whether partition survives will slowly diminish as a result of the habit of co-operation between the communities under the Belfast Agreement's power-sharing provisions for the governance of Northern Ireland. It is striking that, since the achievement of the Belfast Agreement, matters of security rather than the question of the border have been the main source of contention among the parties.

International Influences

The end of the Cold War played a significant role both in the South African transition and in the Northern Ireland peace process. The coming down of the Berlin Wall strongly influenced the initiative of President de Klerk to embark on the pursuit of a negotiated end to apartheid (Guelke 1996). The impact of the end of the Cold War was also a factor in the Republican movement's embrace of a peace strategy and its abandonment of the long war in Northern Ireland (Cox 2006). Similarly, it was a factor influencing the Israeli government's pursuit of the Oslo peace process. Despite the breakdown of this process, there remains wide international support for the concept on which it was based, that the creation of two states constitutes the most viable option for a settlement of the Israeli–Palestinian conflict. But consideration of the impact of external events on deeply divided societies also has to take account of the capacity of the parties in such conflicts to resist international pressures to resolve their differences – a point eloquently made by Churchill when he noted that, after the great cataclysm of the First World War, 'the dreary steeples of Fermanagh and Tyrone' re-appeared and 'the integrity' of the quarrel remained 'undiminished' (Churchill 1941: 319). A prime example in the first decade of this century has been the resistance of the parties in Cyprus to external efforts to resolve the issue on the basis of a longstanding formula of a bi-communal and bi-zonal federation.

But it would be a mistake to treat the difficulty of persuading the parties in deeply divided societies to accept external mediation as a general indication that the conflicts in such societies were, or are, immune to international influences. On the contrary, they play an important role. However, notwithstanding the interests of other states in ending such conflicts, particularly when they have spill-over effects, international influences may exacerbate conflicts as well as contribute to their resolution. Indeed, in justifying their behaviour, the parties to conflicts in deeply divided societies commonly appeal to such international norms as self-determination, territorial integrity, non-intervention and the right of societies to choose their own social system, democracy and human rights. Opposing interpretations of these norms are possible in the context of specific cases, and that helps to sustain the protagonists' belief in the rightness of their cause and to underpin the intractability of conflict, once violence erupts. Recourse for governments, especially since the assault on America on 11 September 2001, is to interpret the outbreak of political violence through the prism of terrorism, thereby denying the insurgents any semblance of legitimacy.

While the end of the Cold War was a factor in the ending of violent conflict in some cases, there is little reason for supposing that this watershed in world affairs spells the end of the problem of deeply divided societies. Indeed, on the contrary, some developments that have occurred as a result of the end of the Cold War seem likely to increase the number of deeply divided societies in the world. In particular, the West's greater tolerance of secession, coupled with the erosion of the non-intervention norm, has created an environment for the multiplication of separatist claims. Insurgents can even entertain the hope that violent suppression by the government may provoke international intervention in their support.

Arguments over the shape and size of polities admit of no easy answer and, though it is entirely predictable that the protagonists in the resulting conflicts will appeal both to democratic and to human rights norms, these may be of little assistance in resolving such questions. But, notwithstanding the West's greater tolerance for secession, international opposition to the widespread sub-division of states remains strong.

Primacy of Internal Solutions

The implications of resistance to a radical redrawing of boundaries are that the primary emphasis will continue to be on internal solutions to the problems of deeply divided societies. While integration offers a route to the avoidance of deep divisions through its emphasis on equal treatment and on measures to tackle discrimination against minorities, it is less persuasive as an approach, once inter-communal violence has taken a hold in an already deeply divided society. The promotion of political accommodation through power-sharing is widely advocated as an effective mechanism for conflict resolution. The consociational model, which includes power-sharing as one of its elements, is especially attractive to parties outside the conflict, as it facilitates external management. At the same time consociationalism is open to the objection that it tends to entrench divisions in the process of seeking to accommodate them, and it has been very widely criticised in practice for this reason.

The territorial division of power, through devolution to regions or the grant of autonomy, provides another way in which the interests of minorities can be addressed so as to retain their support for the polity. But any approach taken by external parties is likely to encounter difficulties if it involves recourse to military force and a continuing external military presence in the society. Agreements that are reached by the parties themselves with a minimum of outside interference stand the best chance of taking root. It is a lesson that those seeking to intervene in other people's conflicts need to bear in mind, whether they are foreign governments or academics promoting the benefits of particular institutional design.

BIBLIOGRAPHY

Aitken, Rob (2007) 'Cementing divisions? An assessment of the impact of international interventions and peace-building policies on ethnic identities and divisions'. *Policy Studies* 28 (3): 247–67.

Aitken, Rob (2010) 'Consociational peace processes and ethnicity: The implications of the Dayton and Good Friday Agreements for ethnic identities and politics in Bosnia-Herzegovina and Northern Ireland'. In Adrian Guelke (ed.), *The Challenges of Ethno-Nationalism: Case Studies in Identity Politics*. Basingstoke: Palgrave Macmillan, pp. 232–53.

Al-Haj, Majid (2004) *Immigration and Ethnic Formation in a Deeply Divided Society: The Case of the 1990s Immigrants from the Former Soviet Union in Israel*. Leiden: Brill.

Allison, Lincoln (2003) 'Ethnicity'. In I. McLean and A. McMillan (eds), *The Concise Oxford Dictionary of Politics*, 2nd edn. Oxford: Oxford University Press.

Almond, Gabriel A. (1956) 'Comparative political systems'. *The Journal of Politics* 18 (3): 391–409.

Autesserre, Séverine (2008) 'The trouble with Congo: How local disputes fuel regional conflict'. *Foreign Affairs* 87 (3): 94–110.

Barker, Bruce (2004) 'Post-conflict policing: Lessons from Uganda 18 years on'. *Journal of Humanitarian Assistance* (April), accessed at: http://www.jha.ac/articles/a138.htm (15 July 2011).

Beckman, James (2007) *Comparative Legal Approaches to Legal Homeland Security and Anti-Terrorism*. Aldershot: Ashgate.

Bell, Christine (2000) *Peace Agreements and Human Rights*. Oxford: Oxford University Press.

Benvenisti, Meron (1990) 'The peace process and intercommunal strife'. In Hermann Giliomee and Jannie Gagiano (eds), *The Elusive Search for Peace: South Africa, Israel and Northern Ireland*. Cape Town: Oxford University Press, pp. 117–31.

Bew, Paul and Gordon Gillespie (1999) *Northern Ireland: A Chronology of the Troubles 1968–1999*, 2nd edn. Dublin: Gill and Macmillan.

Brass, Paul R. (2006) *Forms of Collective Violence: Riots, Pogroms, and Genocide in Modern India*, Gurgaon (Haryana): Three Essays Collective.

Brewer, John D., Adrian Guelke, Ina Hume, Edward Moxon-Browne and Rick Wilford (1988) *The Police, Public Order and the State: Policing in Great Britain, Northern Ireland, the Irish Republic, the USA, Israel, South Africa and China*. Basingstoke: Macmillan Press.

Browning, Christopher R. (2001) *Ordinary Men: Reserve Police Battalion 101 and the Final Solution in Poland*. London: Penguin.

Burg, Steven L. (2003) 'Coercive diplomacy in the Balkans: The U.S. use of force in Bosnia and Kosovo'. In Robert J. Art and Patrick M. Cronin (eds), *The United States and Coercive Diplomacy*. Washington, DC: United States Institute of Peace Press, pp. 57–118.

Cameron, David (2011) 'PM's speech at Munich Security Conference'. *Number 10*, 5 February, accessed at: http://www.number10.gov.uk/news/speeches-and-transcripts/2011/02/pms-speech-at-munich-security-conference-60293 (15 July 2011).

Cassidy, Sarah (2005) 'Schoolgirl banned from wearing Muslim dress wins appeal'. *The Independent*, 2 March.

Cawthra, Gavin (1993) *Policing South Africa: The South African Police and the Transition from Apartheid*. London: Zed Books.

Chalk, Frank and Kurt Jonassohn (1990) *The History and Sociology of Genocide: Analysis and Case Studies*. New Haven, CT: Yale University Press.

Chazan, Naomi, Robert Mortimer, John Ravenhill and Donald Rothchild (1992) *Politics and Society in Contemporary Africa*. Boulder, CO: Lynne Riener Publishers.

Churchill, W. S. (1941) *The Aftermath: Being a Sequel to The World Crisis*. London: Macmillan.

Coakley, John (1992) 'The resolution of ethnic conflict: Towards a typology'. *International Political Science Review* 13 (4), pp. 343–58.

Coakley, John (2004) 'The effectiveness of federal responses to ethnic conflict'. In Adrian Guelke (ed.), *Democracy and Ethnic Conflict: Advancing Peace in Deeply Divided Societies*. Basingstoke: Palgrave Macmillan, pp. 193–210.

Cobban, Alfred (1969) *The Nation State and National Self-Determination*. London: Fontana.

Cockburn, Patrick (2011) 'Egyptian Copts demand end to post-revolution sectarianism'. *The Independent*, 24 May.

Cordell, Karl and Stefan Wolff (2009) *Ethnic Conflict: Causes, Consequences, Responses*. Cambridge: Polity.

Cox, Michael (2006) 'Rethinking the international and Northern Ireland: A defence'. In Michael Cox, Adrian Guelke and Fiona Stephen (eds), *A Farewell to Arms? Beyond the Good Friday Agreement*, 2nd edn. Manchester: Manchester University Press, pp. 427–42.

Craig, W. J. (ed.) (1943) *The Complete Works of William Shakespeare*. London: Oxford University Press.

Crick, Bernard (1990) 'The high price of peace'. In Hermann Giliomee and Jannie Gagiano (eds), *The Elusive Search for Peace: South Africa, Israel and Northern Ireland*. Cape Town: Oxford University Press, pp. 261–75.

Cruise O'Brien, Conor (1962) *To Katanga and Back: A UN Case History*. London: Hutchinson.

Destexhe, Alain (1994–5) 'The third genocide'. *Foreign Policy* 97 (winter), pp. 3–17.

Dow, David R. (2011) 'Death penalty, still racist and arbitrary'. *New York Times*, 8 July.

El Amrani, Issandr (2011) 'Is there a Libya?' *London Review of Books*, 33 (9), 28 April, pp. 19–20.

English, Richard (2009) *Terrorism: How to Respond*. Oxford: Oxford University Press.

Esman, Milton J. (2004) *An Introduction to Ethnic Conflict*. Cambridge: Polity.

The Federal Death Penalty System: A Statistical Survey (1988–2000) (2000). Washington, DC: US Department of Justice.

Fein, Helen (1990) *Genocide: A Sociological Perspective*. London: Sage.

Fiji Islands Bureau of Statistics (2008) '2007 Census of population and housing'. *Statistics News* 46, 15 October.

Finnegan, William (2001) 'The poison keeper'. *New Yorker*, 15 January.

Fisher, Ian (1999) 'Behind Eritrea–Ethiopia, a "knack for stubbornness"'. *New York Times*, 14 February.

Fisk, Robert (1990) *Pity the Nation: Lebanon at War*. London: Andre Deutsch.

Fuller, Thomas (2011) 'Shinawatras pull off another political magic act'. *New York Times*, 4 July.

General Assembly Resolution 2625 (XXV) (1970) 25 UNGAOR Supp. 26 (A/8026) New York: United Nations.

Ghai, Yash and Jill Cottrell (2008) 'A tale of three constitutions: Ethnicity and politics in Fiji'. In Sujit Choudhry (ed.), *Constitutional Design for Divided Societies: Integration or Accommodation?* Oxford: Oxford University Press, pp. 287–315.

Giliomee, Hermann (2003) *The Afrikaners: Biography of a People*. Cape Town: Tafelberg.

Giliomee, Hermann and Lawrence Schlemmer (1989) *From Apartheid to Nation-Building*. Cape Town: Oxford University Press.

Glenny, Misha (1992) *The Fall of Yugoslavia*. London: Penguin Books.

Goldhagen, Daniel Jonah (1997) *Hitler's Willing Executioners: Ordinary Germans and the Holocaust*. London: Abacus.

Guelke, Adrian (1994) 'The peace process in South Africa, Israel and Northern Ireland'. *Irish Studies in International Affairs* 5, pp. 93–106.

Guelke, Adrian (1996) 'The impact of the end of the Cold War on the South African transition'. *Journal of Contemporary African Studies* 14 (1), pp. 87–100.

Gutierrez, Eric and Saturnino Borras, Jr (2004) *The Moro Conflict: Landlessness and Misdirected State Policies* (Policy Studies 8). Washington, DC: East–West Center Washington.

Hadden, Tom (2004) 'Punishment, amnesty and truth: Legal and political approaches'. In Adrian Guelke (ed.), *Democracy and Ethnic Conflict:*

Advancing Peace in Deeply Divided Societies. Basingstoke: Palgrave Macmillan, pp. 196–217.

Harding, Luke (2010) 'Uzbeks in desperate plea for aid as full horror of ethnic slaughter emerges'. *Observer*, 20 June.

Harel-Shalev, Ayelet (2010) *The Challenge of Sustaining Democracy in Deeply Divided Societies: Citizenship, Rights, and Ethnic Conflicts in India and Israel*. Lanham, MD: Lexington Books.

Hart, Peter (1998) *The IRA and its enemies: Violence and community in Cork, 1916–1923*. Oxford: Clarendon Press.

Havlová, Radka (2005) 'The "velvet" divorce of Czechoslovakia as a solution to a conflict of nationalisms'. In Adrian Guelke (ed.), *Democracy and Ethnic Conflict: Advancing Peace in Deeply Divided Societies*. Basingstoke: Palgrave Macmillan, pp. 103–117.

Hays, Constance L. (1988) '11 guardian angels arrested in a dispute with 2 officers'. *New York Times*, 13 July.

Heraclides, Alexis (1991) *The Self-Determination of Minorities in International Politics*. London: Frank Cass.

Hill, Andrew and Andrew White (2008) 'The flying of Israeli flags in Northern Ireland'. *Identities*, 15 (1): 31–50.

Horowitz, Donald L. (2000) *Ethnic Groups in Conflict*. Berkeley and Los Angeles: University of California Press.

Horowitz, Donald L. (2001) 'The Northern Ireland Agreement: Clear, consociational, and risky'. In John McGarry (ed.), *Northern Ireland and the Divided World: Post-Agreement Northern Ireland in Comparative Perspective*. Oxford: Oxford University Press, pp. 89–108.

Horowitz, Donald L. (2002) *The Deadly Ethnic Riot*. Berkeley and Los Angeles: University of California Press.

Huntington, Samuel P. (1993) 'The clash of civilizations?' *Foreign Affairs*, 72 (3) (summer): 22–49.

Hutchinson, John and Anthony D. Smith (1996) 'Introduction'. In John Hutchinson and Anthony D. Smith (eds), *Ethnicity*. Oxford: Oxford University Press, pp. 3–14.

Independent Commission on Policing in Northern Ireland (1999) *A New Beginning: Policing in Northern Ireland: The Report of the Independent Commission on Policing* (Patten Report). Belfast: Independent Commission on Policing in Northern Ireland, 9 September.

Jenkins, Paul (2009) 'Holder, race and Obama's 10% of the white Alabama vote'. *Huffington Post*, 21 February, accessed at: http://www.huffingtonpost.com/paul-jenkins/holder-race-and-obamas-10_b_168852.html (15 July 2011).

Kumar, Radha (2005) *Making Peace with Partition*. New Delhi: Penguin.

Kumar, Radha (ed.) (2009) *Negotiating Peace in Deeply Divided Societies: A Set of Simulations*, New Delhi: SAGE India.

Kuper, Leo (1981) *Genocide*. Harmondsworth: Penguin.

Lawson, Stephanie (1990) 'The myth of cultural homogeneity and its implications for chiefly power and politics in Fiji'. *Comparative Studies in Society and History* 32 (4): 795–821.

Leff, Carol Skalnik (1996) *The Czech and Slovak Republics: Nation versus State*. Boulder, CO: Westview.

Lemkin, Raphael (1944) *Axis Rule in Occupied Europe*. Washington, DC: Carnegie Endowment for International Peace.

Lijphart, Arend (1968) 'Typologies of democratic systems'. *Comparative Political Studies* 1 (April): 3–44.

Lijphart, Arend (1975) *The Politics of Accommodation: Pluralism and Democracy in the Netherlands*, 2nd edn. Berkeley: University of California Press.

Lijphart, Arend (1977) *Democracy in Plural Societies: A Comparative Exploration*. New Haven and London: Yale University Press.

Lijphart, Arend (1994) 'Prospects for power sharing in the new South Africa'. In Andrew Reynolds (ed.), *Election '94 South Africa: The Campaigns, Results and Future Prospects*. London: James Currey, pp. 221–31.

Lipset, Seymour Martin (1983) *Political Man: The Social Bases of Politics*. London: Heinemann.

Lustick, Ian S. (1979) 'Stability in deeply divided societies: Consociationalism versus control'. *World Politics*, 31 (3), pp. 325–44.

McCloskey, Stephen (2000) 'Introduction: East Timor from European to Third World colonialism'. In Paul Hainsworth and Stephen McCloskey (eds), *The East Timor Question: The Struggle for Independence from Indonesia*. London: I. B. Tauris, pp. 1–16.

McGarry, John and Brendan O'Leary (1993) 'Introduction'. In John McGarry and Brendan O'Leary (eds), *The Politics of Ethnic Conflict Regulation*. London and New York: Routledge, pp. 1–40.

McGarry, John and Brendan O'Leary (2008) 'Iraq's constitution of 2005: Liberal consociation as political prescription'. In Sujit Choudhry (ed.), *Constitutional Design for Divided Societies: Integration or Accommodation?* Oxford: Oxford University Press, pp. 342–68.

McGuire, Maria (1973) *To Take Arms: A Year in the Provisional IRA*. London: Macmillan.

McKenzie, W. J. M. (1975) *Power, Violence, Decision*. Harmondsworth: Penguin.

Mayall, James (1971) *Africa: The Cold War and after*. London: Elek Books.

Mitchell, Thomas (2000) *Native vs. Settler: Ethnic Conflict in Israel/Palestine, Northern Ireland and South Africa*. Westport, CT: Greenwood Press.

Moreno, Luis (2006) 'Scotland, Catalonia, Europanization and the "Moreno question"'. *Scottish Affairs* 54 (winter), accessed at: http://www.scottishaffairs.org/onlinepub/sa/moreno_sa54_winter06.html (15 July 2011).

Moriarty, Gerry (2010) 'PSNI's 50–50 system "should end in 2011"'. *The Irish Times*, 18 October.

Morris, Benny (1987) *The Birth of the Palestinian Refugee Problem, 1947–1949*. Cambridge: Cambridge University Press.

Murray, Christina and Richard Simeon (2008) 'Recognition without empowerment: Minorities in a democratic South Africa'. In Sujit Choudhry (ed.), *Constitutional Design for Divided Societies: Integration or Accommodation?* Oxford: Oxford University Press, pp. 409–37.

Nagle, John and Mary-Alice C. Clancy (2010) *Shared Society or Benign Apartheid? Understanding Peace-Building in Divided Societies*. Basingstoke: Palgrave Macmillan.

Nordlinger, Eric (1972) *Conflict Regulation in Divided Societies*. Cambridge, MA: Center for International Affairs, Harvard University.

Nossiter, Adam (2011) 'Election fuels deadly clashes in Nigeria'. *New York Times*, 24 April.

O'Flynn, Ian (2006) *Deliberative Democracy and Deeply Divided Societies*. Edinburgh: Edinburgh University Press.

Paterson, Tony (2009) 'The fall of the Wall: For some there's little to celebrate'. *The Independent on Sunday*, 8 November.

Pavković, Aleksandar with Peter Radan (2007) *Creating New States: Theory and Practice of Secession*. Aldershot: Ashgate.

Peleg, Ilan (2007) *Democratizing the Hegemonic State: Political Transformation in the Age of Identity*. Cambridge and New York: Cambridge University Press.

Premdas, Ralph R. (1995) *Ethnic Conflict and Development: The Case of Fiji*. Aldershot: Avebury.

Priestland, Gerald (1974) *The Future of Violence*. London: Hamish Hamilton.

Prunier, Gérard (1995) *The Rwanda Crisis 1959–1994: History of a Genocide*. London: Hurst and Company.

Ramesh, Randeep (2007) 'Surprise landslide in Indian state election'. *Guardian*, 12 May.

Rex, John (1997) 'The nature of ethnicity in the project of migration'. In Montserrat Guibernau and John Rex (eds), *The Ethnicity Reader: Nationalism, Multiculturalism and Migration*. Cambridge: Polity Press, pp. 269–83.

Richmond, Oliver P. (1998) *Mediating in Cyprus: The Cypriot Communities and the United Nations*. London: Frank Cass.

Rosenbaum, H. Jon and Peter C. Sederberg (1976) 'Vigilantism: An analysis of establishment violence'. In H. Jon Rosenbaum and Peter C. Sederberg (eds), *Vigilante Politics*. Philadelphia: University of Pennsylvania Press, pp. 4–29.

Rudd, Kevin (2008) 'Text of PM's "sorry" address'. *The Age Online*, 13 February, accessed at: http://www.theage.com.au/articles/2008/02/12/1202760291188.html (15 July 2011).

Ryle, John (1998) 'A sorry apology from Clinton'. *Guardian*, 13 April.

Sachs, Albie (1973) *Justice in South Africa*, London: Heinemann for Sussex University Press.

Safran, William (2010) 'Multiculturalism, ethnicity and the nation-state'. In André Lecours and Luis Moreno (eds), *Nationalism and Democracy: Dichotomies, Complementarities, Oppositions*. London and New York: Routledge, pp. 16–37.

Scally, Derek (2011) 'Charismatic leaders winning votes with simple answers to complex questions'. *The Irish Times*, 26 April.

Schofield, Victoria (2000) *Kashmir in Conflict: India, Pakistan and the Unfinished War*. London: I. B. Tauris.

Schulze, Kirsten (2002) 'Laskar Jihad and the conflict in Ambon'. *Brown Journal of World Affairs* 9 (1): 57–70.

Sharpe, Tom (1973) *Riotous Assembly*. London: Pan Books.

Shaw, Mark (2002) *Crime and Policing in Post-Apartheid South Africa: Transforming under Fire*. London: Hurst and Co.

Sheehy, Kevin (2008) *More Questions than Answers: Reflections on a Life in the RUC*. Dublin: Gill and Macmillan.

Sidiropoulos, Elizabeth (ed.) (1997) *South Africa Survey 1996/97*. Johannesburg: South African Institute of Race Relations.

Simpson, John and Edmund Weiner (eds) (1989) *Oxford English Dictionary*, 2nd edn, vol. 19. Oxford: Clarendon Press.

Sisk, Timothy D. (1995) *Democratization in South Africa: The Elusive Social Contract*. Princeton, NJ: Princeton University Press.

Smith, David (2011) 'Laurent Gbagdo's humiliating fall'. *Guardian*, 12 April.

Soares, Claire (2009) '156 dead as Muslim uprising hits China'. *Independent*, 7 July.

Steinberg, Jonny (2008) *Thin Blue: The Unwritten Rules of Policing South Africa*. Johannesburg and Cape Town: Jonathan Ball Publishers.

Taylor, Rupert (2009) 'Introduction: The promise of consociational theory'. In Rupert Taylor (ed.), *Consociational Theory: McGarry and O'Leary and the Northern Ireland conflict*. London and New York: Routledge, pp. 1–11.

Thompson, Della (1995) *The Concise Oxford Dictionary*, 9th edn. Oxford: Clarendon Press.

Tolland, James (1997) *Adolf Hitler*. Ware, Hertfordshire: Wordsworth Editions.

Van Schalkwyk, Rex (1999) 'Gradually being brought to heel'. *Frontiers of Freedom*. Johannesburg: South African Institute of Race Relations, Issue No. 21, third quarter, pp. 5–7.

Varshney, Ashutosh (2002) *Ethnic Conflict and Civil Life: Hindus and Muslims in India*. New Haven and London: Yale University Press.

Weitzer, Ronald (1990) *Transforming Settler States: Communal Conflict and Internal Security in Northern Ireland and Zimbabwe*. Berkeley: University of California Press.

Westmoreland, Ken (2009) *A Pretty Unfair Place: East Timor Ten Years after Self-Determination*. London: Lafaek Press.

Whyte, John (1983) 'How much discrimination was there under the Unionist regime, 1921–1968?' In Tom Gallagher and James O'Connell (eds), *Contemporary Irish Studies*. Manchester: Manchester University Press, pp. 1–35.

Wirsing, Robert G. (2004) 'The autonomy puzzle: Territorial solutions to the Kashmir conflict'. In Adrian Guelke (ed.), *Democracy and Ethnic Conflict: Advancing Peace in Deeply Divided Societies*. Basingstoke: Palgrave Macmillan, pp. 80–102.

Wolf, Martin (2011) 'We should declare an end to our disastrous war on drugs'. *Financial Times*, 4 and 5 June.

Wright, Frank (1987) *Northern Ireland: A Comparative Analysis*. Dublin: Gill and Macmillan.

Wright, Frank (1996) *Two Lands on One Soil: Ulster Politics Before Home Rule*. Dublin: Gill and Macmillan.

Zartman, I. William (2008) 'The timing of peace initiatives: Hurting stalemates and ripe moments'. In John Darby and Roger Mac Ginty (eds), *Contemporary Peacemaking: Conflict, Peace Processes and Post-War Reconstruction*, 2nd edn. Basingstoke: Palgrave Macmillan, pp. 22–35.

INDEX